My Long Island

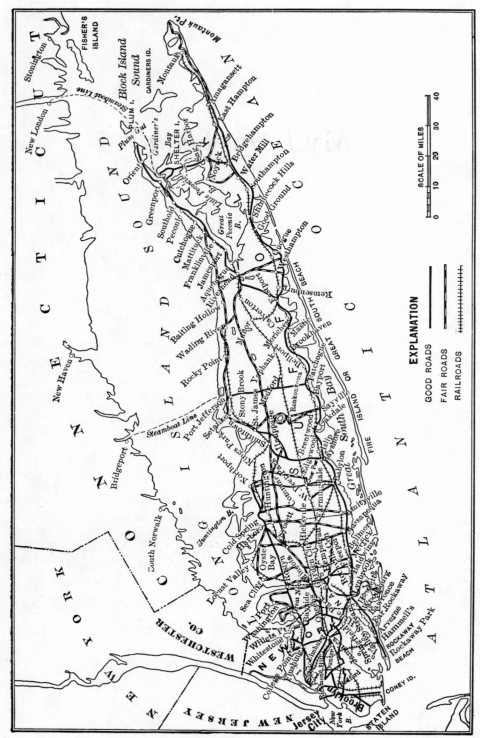

"Long Island in contour is very like a whale." From *Unique Long Island* (Long Island Railroad Company, 1899)

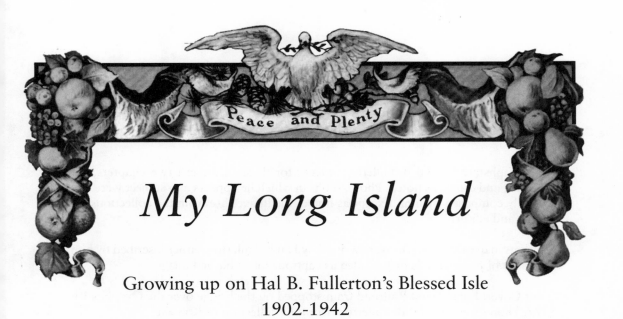

My Long Island

Growing up on Hal B. Fullerton's Blessed Isle
1902-1942

ELEANOR F. FERGUSON

EDITED BY ANNE NAUMAN

Scrub Oak Press ♦ Las Vegas, NV

Photographs are by Hal B. Fullerton, except for those in the last two chapters, studio portraits, and others as noted. Photographs in which he appears as a subject were almost certainly composed by him. Except as noted, the images are from the collections of the author and editor.

Captions in quotation marks were written by Hal B. Fullerton, either inscribed by him on the backs of photographs or provided as captions for published images.

Front Cover: Long Island Railroad train stopped on the bridge over the Carmans River, 1897. Photograph by Hal B. Fullerton, from the collection of Ron Ziel.

Back Cover: The author with a giant cabbage grown on the Experimental Farm at Wading River, 1906. Photograph by Hal B. Fullerton.

Typeset by Type-Right
Pre-press production, including half-tones, by Suburban Graphics, Inc.
Printed by Chuck Pick Printing, Inc.
Book and cover designed by Anne Nauman. Cover art was executed by Hal B. Fullerton for *The Lure of the Land* (Edith Loring Fullerton, Long Island Railroad Company, 1907).

Scrub Oak Press, P.O. Box 34691, Las Vegas, NV 89133

Library of Congress Catalog Card Number 93-84734
ISBN 0-9637126-1-6

Printed and Bound in the United States of America

For my father and mother

Hal B. and Edith Loring Fullerton

who gave me such beautiful and happy
—and interesting—
growing-up years

Reflections

Contents

Editor's Preface

My Long Island began as an informal memoir and family history written by my mother, Eleanor Fullerton Ferguson. It was originally titled *As I Remember It* and was privately printed in 1978. In it she described a remarkable life lived close to the earth on rural Long Island in the early 1900s.

She wrote *As I Remember It* in stream-of-consciousness fashion, her recollections taking her from subject to subject, from decade to decade and back again. It was not always easy to follow. But it was warm and funny, evocative and engrossing. I was sure that this extraordinary story would appeal to a much wider audience if it could be organized into chapters, shortened a bit, and generously embellished with vintage photographs from the family trove. Our large collection of her father's photographs included images that would be uniquely appropriate as illustrations for the book.

Three years ago, with my mother's blessing, I undertook the task of organizing, abridging and illustrating. I edited gently, pruned carefully, corrected here and there, and sorted through hundreds of photographs. I added little, although it seemed that I moved virtually every paragraph. Despite the changes wrought in the course of 22 drafts, *My Long Island* is faithful to the author's own words and the book remains uniquely Eleanor Ferguson's work.

She lived with us for several months at our little oasis in southern Nevada's Mojave Desert. During that time she carefully reviewed every change I had made. The rereading of her own book, together with our many discussions, brought to mind some additional details which she added to the manuscript.

As we discussed possible titles for this revision, she remarked, "We could call it *Life with Father*." Her story is indeed dominated by the dynamic figure of her father, Hal B. Fullerton, flamboyant publicity man, talented and prolific photographer, agricultural expert, writer, lecturer, visionary and, above all, devoted family man. As a special agent for the Long Island Railroad, HBF demonstrated Long Island's agricultural potential by clearing so-called "waste land" and creating two thriving experimental farms where he grew 1000 varieties of plants. Eleanor Fullerton grew up on the second farm. Her close bond with her father pervades this entire book. It is, in fact, as much his biography as it is her autobiography. Her child's-eye view of HBF puts a new perspective on the personality of a man who wrote an important chapter in the history of Long Island, his "Blessed Isle."

An exhibition of HBF's photographs and memorabilia was presented in 1990-91 by the Suffolk County Historical Society. In abbreviated form, it has been moved to a series of other locations on the Island as a traveling exhibit. In conjunction with the original exhibition, a well-researched study of HBF's photographic work was written by Charles Sachs: *The Blessed Isle: Hal B. Fullerton and his Image of Long Island, 1897-1927.* Through these efforts, a new generation of Long Islanders has become acquainted with HBF and his unique contributions to the Island's development.

I am sure we speak for the entire Fullerton family when we express our gratitude to the Society, particularly its Director, Wallace W. Broege, and Charles Sachs, for this recognition of HBF's work. We are also grateful to Wallace Broege for providing us with prints of several images from the Society's extensive HBF collection and for his helpfulness in many other aspects of this project.

We acknowledge with thanks the contributions of Kim Sakowski and Lisa Donato of Suburban Graphics and LynnAnn Martin of Type-Right. Their interest and enthusiasm, as well as their expertise, were greatly appreciated.

The rest of Eleanor Ferguson's progeny–son Bill, who is surely smiling upon us from the Great Beyond, daughter Edith, and grandchildren Don, Judy, Doug, Eric, Margaret, Bill, Rob, Marcy, Pam and Paula–encouraged us and provided moral support, for which we thank them. Margaret was especially helpful with her comments on the text.

Chuck deserves special mention for his patience and good humor as I monopolized the computer, wore out a printer, depleted the bank account, and generally cluttered up the house with stacks of printouts and photographs.

I particularly owe thanks to the author, my mother, for her enthusiastic cooperation in this venture, for her forbearance as I endlessly shuffled her words around, and especially for her patience during the interminable publication process. She is, at this writing, a frail but eminently lucid 91-year-old who looks forward to holding this book in her hand.

Clark County, Nevada   A. N.

Author's Preface

When I started this book in 1968 my only aim was to write down some family history for my children and grandchildren. I have been very much surprised through the years to find other people interested in it.

I can understand those who are real Long Islanders and interested in Long Island history, for my father made a lot of Long Island history and I lived through it while he was making it.

Others have said that it tells of another way of life and reminds them of their grandparents' stories. My own 91 years have been very eventful years for the world has seen many astonishing changes.

This revised edition of *As I Remember It* has been edited and substantially reorganized by my daughter Anne, and it omits a lot of purely personal matter that cannot interest any but the children and grandchildren for whom I originally wrote.

I remember my Dad's "Blessed Isle" as it was in my young days with great nostalgia. I am glad I had the privilege of living then.

Williston, Vermont   E.F.F.

Hal B. Fullerton in the early 1900s.

Prologue: My Father, Hal B. Fullerton

My father was christened Harry Barry Fullerton. This must have pleased Sam Barry and Harry Ibetson—the friends his father so honored—but it gave young Harry trouble when he went west as a young man. He felt that the name Harry Barry would not set well with the rugged gentry of the Texas plains, so he became Hal B. Fullerton and was so known to the end of his days. Not only known but rather well-known, for Dad was not a man to be lost in the shuffle. He was definitely what would be called a colorful character. When Ron Ziel was researching his book on the Long Island Railroad, *Steel Rails to the Sunrise,* he said that in his travels around the Island he ran across three legends everywhere: the train wreck at Calverton when the Shelter Island Express went through the pickle works, the 1938 hurricane, and Hal B. Fullerton.

A year before he and my mother were married, Dad became a Special Agent for the Long Island Railroad. He was a publicity man—a perfect job, for Dad thrived on the public and publicity. Long Island became his to explore and exploit, to love and to laud, to make known to the whole world as the Blessed Isle.

His explorations were extensive. He was a cyclist, a member of the League of American Wheelmen and that exclusive cycling club, the Whirling Dervishes. He was a photographer and a member of the Brooklyn Academy of Photography. He had discovered Long Island in these capacities long before LIRR President Baldwin gave him the job of "Fullertonizing Long Island."

With his five-by-seven or his eleven-by-fourteen camera strapped to his bicycle, he went looking for photographs. These were not the easy days of photography. No light meters, no fast film and fast shutters, and certainly not the instant magic of today's automatic marvels. The eleven-by-fourteen he referred to as "the doghouse." Both cameras required heavy tripods which had to be carted along. They were bellows cameras and used glass plates in heavy frames. All the roads he traveled were dirt roads and this meant, according to season, deep sand, dry ruts, muddy ruts or dust. But he got beautiful photographs and won many a prize.

Dad's mission for the LIRR was to prove to the world that his Blessed Isle could produce prodigious crops, even on scrub oak waste and sandy pine barrens. He succeeded beyond everyone's expectations. He cleared the so-called waste land and created two thriving experimental farms, one in Wading River and one in Medford, where he grew more than 1000 varieties of fruits and vegetables.

He spread the news in his own flamboyant and extravagant style. He wore his heart on his sleeve. He may have been overenthusiastic in his loyalties, he may have turned a blind eye to some of the discrepancies in his vision of Long Island, but his sincerity and his fierce enthusiasm and his ability to *talk* that enthusiasm made him a man to be listened to and a man to remember.

Dad was not a large man—five feet seven according to his driver's license, but as I remember him he was the same height as I, and I am five feet five—of slight build, permanently weather-tanned, with a shock of snow-white hair and a cigarette-smoke-stained mustache, the ends of which he twirled when deep in thought. It was not a long, Kaiser Wilhelm type of mustache but it had a definite upswing. This gave him a look of always being on his toes, especially when he was really wound up and his hair seemed to stand on end of its own accord.

Wound up! That was my Dad. He was permanently wound up from the time I first knew him—and, I assume, prior to that—to about the age of seventy when his work was done and his fires burned out and he became a rather sad little old man. I suppose this is understandable—nothing can burn indefinitely with the fine incandescent blaze that was his, and when such a fire goes out it leaves only ashes. I would rather not think of him that way. I would rather remember the days of his blazing.

Family Tales

Dad told us, or anyone else who happened to be around, many tales of his ancestors, but these, like most of his stories, were subject to revision with each telling. He was a marvelous raconteur, could hold an audience entranced, and believed that a good story should never be spoiled by a slavish adherence to the facts. If a little embroidery made a good story better, why hesitate to embroider?

There hung a portrait at home of James Fullerton who, Dad claimed, was an Admiral in the British Navy. (Take first grain of salt.) He made port in Ireland one fine day, saw a gorgeous girl with blue eyes and black hair and refused to sail until she married him.

The story continued—when the British Admiralty decreed that he should retire, James was outraged that they should so treat a man still in his prime. He packed up the Irish wife and whatever progeny they had at that time and left Great Britain in a huff. He could not, however, turn his back on the Empire so he emigrated to Halifax, Nova Scotia, and settled there, still under the British flag. In his old age, he had his portrait painted (by Rembrandt Peale, according to Dad). Dad claimed that the crusty old gentleman would not accept the painting until the artist pulled aside the drapery of the background and painted in a fort on a headland with the British flag flying on the turret. My sister sold this portrait, to my sorrow. It hung in the dining room all the days of my childhood.

The records reveal that James was indeed a seafaring man, but was the Captain of the armed sloop *Wren* rather than an Admiral in the Queen's Navee. Furthermore, it appears that the portrait was actually of James' son, also called James. This second James was also a seafaring man and was Captain of the coasting schooner *Halifax* and later of the *Morning Star*. In 1792 the *Morning Star* was part of a fleet of fifteen ships that took 1200 liberated slaves and other free blacks to Sierra Leone for resettlement. The second James married Lydia Cobb of Liverpool,

Nova Scotia, who was directly descended from Plymouth Pilgrims—Richard Warren who came over on the *Mayflower* and Robert Bartlett who arrived on the *Ann.*

Lydia's father, Jabez Cobb, was also a sea captain. According to the records, he was captured by pirates in 1759 but was rescued by his older brother, Captain John Cobb, who had been pursuing the privateer in an armed ship. Dad's version of this episode revolved around a grand old Masonic watch that was kept in a curio cabinet in our living room. It was quite a thing with the Masonic emblems on its face. According to Dad's legend, when this seafaring ancestor was on the point of being forced to walk the plank, the pirate captain charged up on deck and called a halt to the proceedings. It seems he had been going through his captive's effects and came across the Masonic watch. Lo and behold, he too was a Mason and no fellow Mason would suffer at his hands.

The second James Fullerton and Lydia had a son, also named James, who moved from Halifax to Boston in 1809. He was a steel importer and the last Fullerton to have a head for business. An 1889 newspaper clipping refers to this third James as "one of the old-time merchant princes." His first wife died in childbirth with their first child, James John. We had a portrait of James John which usually hung in a fairly dark corner. He had been painted holding his derby hat upside-down in his lap and Dad always referred to him as "Old Lend Me Five Cents."

The third James remarried and had five more children. The youngest was my grandfather, William King Reynolds Fullerton. William spent most of his life in Cincinnati in the hardware business, and that is where he met Frances Cornelia Lyon, my grandmother. As for Frances Cornelia's family, we have some of Dad's finest salty tales. These were among his favorites and repeated ad infinitum.

To begin with—and I am telling it just as he told it—Frances Cornelia's father, Jonathan Lyon, was a bookkeeper from Paris, France, who emigrated to America. In tidewater Virginia he met Matilda Garde, a cigarette roller from Madrid, and they were married. He was 16 and she was 14. They went west in a covered wagon and "built the first log cabin in Cincinnati." Frances Cornelia was the fifteenth of their sixteen children.

According to another tale of these pioneering grandparents, Jonathan was working his land one day when he heard shots from the house inside the stockade. Cutting his horses loose, he sprinted to the rescue, knowing it was an Indian raid and hoping he would be in time. When he got there he found seven dead Indians and the rest retreating over the stockade while Matilda was calmly reloading the musket "with Oliver on her left arm."

Jonathan left his mark on young grandson Harry, who had to read the Bible aloud to his grandfather, a chapter a day. And when they finished he started all over again. I will say my Dad had odd bits of biblical knowledge that came out in odd ways. A favorite ejaculation of his was "Bildad the Shuhite!" Out of context it

The Fullerton christening dress, worn by Loring in 1908

does have a nice ring but I was quite surprised to meet Bildad when I got to read the Book of Job at a much later date. In one of Dad's articles he refers to "that great biblical grain speculator, Joseph."

According to Dad, at the age of ninety-five Jonathan walked two miles—or perhaps it was five—to beat up the editor of the local paper who had printed the story of Jonathan's life. An invasion of privacy? Or just a good tale for Dad's collection?

Matilda never learned to read or write. She died at the age of ninety-six while knitting quietly, and Jonathan died at ninety-eight while reading the Bible. They had been married for eighty-two years.

William and Frances Cornelia Fullerton had four children. Harry Barry (Hal B.), the eldest, was born on August 15, 1857, seven years after William and Frances were married. He was not a robust baby so they had him baptized—or christened— by "every minister who came through town." This was no doubt to keep him in good standing but it must have been a joy to Frances Cornelia to dress him in the christening dress, which we still have—a lovely little off-the-shoulder number with tiny puffed sleeves, voluminous skirts and many rows of tiny tucks.

Lily, the second child, died at the age of three. The next child, James, became a traveling agent for the Mexican Central Railroad. The only tale I remember of him was that he was a crack shot on some fabulous rifle team in international competition. He disturbed everyone because he sighted with the wrong eye and eventually it came out that he was blind in the other eye. The fourth child, Clarence—always called the Kid—was thirteen years younger than Dad. He was the flamboyant type, more like Hal B. than James. Clarence worked on the Panama Canal. He received some kind of recognition because he lasted for a year without dying of yellow fever.

Childhood in Cincinnati must have been a typical small-town and country life. Gardening and farming were the order of the day and Dad apparently soaked this up. In later years, when he became an "agricultural expert," he always said that he just remembered the way things were done in his youth.

He told a tale of waking up in the middle of the night when he was quite young and hearing surreptitious noises that he knew were none of his business. I don't know if he knew at the time, or learned later, that this was Underground Railroad activity, and escaped slaves were being helped through on their way to Canada. It seems to me this was at his grandfather's house.

He also told of seeing General Custer. It seems that the word went around that Custer was coming through town and Dad saw it all from the top of a fence. The troop came by at a full gallop, yelling the Cavalry yell and with scarlet kerchiefs streaming. He said it looked as if every man's throat had been cut and the impression was so tremendous that young Hal fell backwards off the fence. I feel that no salt is needed here. I'm sure Custer was the kind of man to stage just such a ride through town.

Dad's mother died soon after Clarence's birth, when Hal was thirteen. As she lay on her deathbed she urged William to marry her dear friend, Sarah Mehitabel Simmons of Duxbury, Massachusetts, which he did. She was a well-loved stepmother to the three boys. She visited us often in my early days. She was a busy little lady, dressed in crackling black taffeta with ruching around neck and cuffs. Every night she put her thin white hair in hairpins so it lay in neat ridges which fascinated me. Dad nicknamed her Grandma Busybody but we just called her Grandma Busy and loved her dearly. She died during one of her visits to us and even during her final illness she sat up each night to put her hair up in the hairpins.

In 1875 Dad entered M.I.T. and studied civil engineering. He left after a year, claiming "it was unfair to the Kid." Details behind this I do not know. Apparently Dad was either devoted to Clarence or had a feeling of responsibility for him. Of the sixty-six regular members who started with Dad's class, twenty-four graduated in 1879 at the first commencement exercises held at M.I.T. This was also the class that chose the school colors, cardinal and silver gray.

A class reunion yearbook was published after their twenty-fifth reunion. The Directory and Personal Sketch section of this volume contains the following

Grandma Busy, 1910

resume of his life as he wrote it for them in 1904. This is probably the most accurate account of his early life we could ever find, although I do feel he got carried away in a few fields, especially his sporting accomplishments.

In 1877 to the oil fields as inside Superintendent of an oil company; in 1878 to Texas as general utility man in cottonseed oil mill; 1880-81 hydraulic engineer, Holyoke Water Power Co.; 1881 asst. engineer Canal and Water Division, Richmond and Allegheny Railroad, surveying the dam at Lynchburg, then four years in the paper business in the New England circuit; 1886 Paymaster for a New England cotton mill; 1887 buyer and manager, Seeger and Guernsey Co., Exporters and Importers; 1890 Asst. Treasurer of same company; 1891-92 machinery manager Mexico City Branch; 1893-97 Vice President of the same company stationed in New York; since 1897 Special Agent of the Passenger Dept., Long Island Railroad.

Personal sketch. I am the author of many pamphlets on Mexico, books on Good Roads, Cyclopedia of Manufactures and Products of the United States, articles on Photography, Bicycling, Automobiling, Yachting, Fishing, Hunting, Poultry, Asparagus, Home Making, Subterranean Water Sources, Flower Culture, Oiling Roadbeds of Railroads and Highways, Manual Education of Children, etc.

I am an outdoor man: baseball, football, skating, scootering, long distance running, walking, wrestling, revolver shooting, lariat casting, horseback, bicycling, automobiling, photography (sport and art), flower culture, poultry raising (with financial success); traveled over each and every one of these United States, Canada, New Brunswick, Mexico, Central and South America and the West Indies, for business and pleasure.

For hobbies I have good roads, photography and flowers. Have been shot, stabbed, thoroughly broken, skull fractured, arms broken (right twice, left once), left leg once and one rib; was killed (so doctors and papers said) in famous Fournier automobile accident in 1901, scalped, leg and eye mashed, etc., but still have all members in good working order.

The oil fields he mentions here were, as I recall, the Pennsylvania oil fields, and he spoke of Bradford, Pennsylvania. The two years in Texas gave him limitless material for tall tales. Dad fancied the role of Rugged Pioneer and he made much of being in Texas "when every man was his own policeman." He often referred to himself as a Texan and wore a semi-ten-gallon hat to the end of his days. While I doubt that he rode the range, and I know he never roped a steer, he certainly absorbed the aura of the Old West and it became a part of his image. He secured an appointment as Deputy Sheriff and always wore the badge on his belt. There was always a revolver around the house and I have a nagging recollection of him wearing this in a holster.

He certainly acquired the cowboy crouch and he dropped to his heels with the greatest of ease. Other people just stood till their backs ached but Dad was very comfortable crouched in the shade of a tree, gesticulating with the ever-present cigarette in its short holder, and always talking, while the listener stood there spellbound. Dad indeed had a silver tongue.

Another result of his Texas days (he said) was his way of getting up in the morning. He was out of bed and on his feet the instant he was awake. His explanation of this was that when you slept in the open with a saddle for a pillow the rattlers would crawl up next to you for warmth. It therefore behooved you to get to your feet fast and put some distance between you and your sleeping place and *then* look to see if you had company.

There was the tale of breaking a leg while he was alone out on the prairie, of getting back into the saddle and of the horse getting him back to civilization.

If, as the autobiographical sketch says, he worked in New England during the early 1880s, this must have been the time he married May (Mary? Molly?) Pierce. I never knew anything about this marriage until one day, when I must have been

"Courtyard of the School of Art." Mexico City, c. 1892

about twelve, there was a subdued bustle around the house and Dad went off for a day or two and we heard that his first wife's mother had died. I doubt that there was any intention to keep this a secret from us. It just never came up. I believe that his wife went to Mexico with him and it is my impression that she died there.

Of his years in Mexico, Dad had many tales. One was about President Porfirio Diaz and the *pastillas de goma*. As an importer, Dad was in a position to favor El Presidente, and El Presidente had a sweet tooth and a passion for gumdrops. Therefore, Dad imported *pastillas de goma* in quantity and delivered them to the presidential palace.

He traveled around extensively as Machinery Manager for the Seeger and Guernsey Company. He never did become fluent in Spanish but obviously learned enough to do his work. The big landowners may have had some English and it was they who bought the machinery. The farm workers were terrified of the monsters. One tale dealt with a threshing machine that had been ordered. Dad went along to see it set up and put into operation. The workers were not about to use the devilish thing and were persuaded with difficulty to try it. Shortly it came to a screeching halt when someone heaved a pitchfork into the works, intending no doubt to spear the resident devil. All work had to cease until repairs could be made, and Dad figured something more was needed. He rode around the villages and finally found a local priest who, for an adequate donation of tequila, was willing to come and bless the Gringo machine. Once this was done and the repairs were made, the thresher went into operation.

Water carriers, Mexico, c. 1892

He got into some unusual parts of the country. He loved Yucatan and said it had the perfect climate, spring all year round. The Mayan ruins fascinated him. He told a tale of a labyrinth that the natives feared. He fastened his lariat to a rock near the entrance and went in as far as his rope would reach but he did not dare go farther without something to guide him back. At that, he was afraid someone might cut the rope. They were not enthusiastic about strangers among their ruins. The stone head we still have came from a ruined temple there. An old newspaper clipping describes many more Mexican relics that he later gave to the Museum of Natural History in Springfield, Massachusetts.

He always carried his camera and took beautiful pictures. My sister Hope sent the best of his Mexican pictures to the American Museum of Natural History in New York after his death so they are safe but probably buried in the archives.

The pageantry of this Catholic-Indian country delighted Dad's artistic soul. He had many photographs of processions. The Easter celebration must have been extraordinary when they reenacted the whole story of the Crucifixion. Whether this went on in every village or only in Mexico City I don't know, but it was a time of great religious fervor. The choice of the man to take the part of Christ was of great moment. At the time, he must really have been Christ in their eyes. In earlier times they carried similitude to its ultimate end and actually crucified this proxy Christ but by Dad's day the man was merely tied to the cross for a token length of time.

He brought back opals in quantity and said he gave them away freely to his friends. He also brought back a whole bag of tortillas but these he kept for himself. Apparently he loved them. Opals always figured in our lives and Mother had many. She had a lovely opal ring that he gave her when I was born. This she gave to me on my wedding day and I treasured it. But, as opals will, it shattered one day and was gone.

While in Mexico City, Dad lived in what I suppose was a boarding house— a pension—run by the Allens. Two nieces of the landlady came to visit from Bristol, Pennsylvania, and that is how my mother and father met. Oddly enough, one of the visiting nieces was also named May (or Maisie) Pierce, but it was the other, Edith Loring Jones, who later married the dashing Hal B.

At the time the girls came to stay with their aunt, my mother was only sixteen. We have a picture of her in that era and she looked like a sweet and gentle girl. Dad must have seemed quite the dashing caballero to her and he was no doubt romantic. He was always given to "gestures" and he brought the girls flowers from the flower market. Black pansies grew big and velvety in the floating gardens of Xochimilco and these he brought to Mother. We had black pansies in the garden for years. Like the opals, they seemed to spell Mexico.

I remember talk of a ball in Mexico City to which the girls were invited. I don't know if they made their dresses down there or if they carried such finery with them from home, but for this occasion their dresses were trimmed with nosegays of real flowers all over the full skirts. One of them used rosebuds and the other wore violets.

In Dad's tales this Mexican meeting made good material. "I met her in Mexico and it took me six years to persuade her to marry me."

My mother was born October 24, 1876 and was named for her mother's friend Edith Loring Getchell. She was the only child of Eleanor Louise (Nell) Switzer and John Alonzo Jones. John was a traveling salesman of some sort and left wife and child in boarding houses here and there with little attention from him and very little financial support. When my mother was four and a half years old, Eleanor Louise died and her sister Kate Pierce took the child into her home in Bristol. The Pierces had two daughters near Edith's age. Willowmere, the Pierce home where my mother grew up, was a lovely big house overlooking the Delaware River. I vaguely remember the house and its idyllic setting with river scenes framed by big old willow trees.

HBF in Mexican attire, 1893

Aunty Kate was married to Will Pierce, and thereby seems to hang a tale. My cousin Jean told me she understood that Will and Eleanor Switzer had been "very devoted," which suggests that marriage may have been on their minds. But sister Kate cast an eye on Will and found him good, and what Kate wanted Kate got.

What a story could be woven here. Perhaps the dashing John Alonzo came along at this time and bemused Eleanor long enough for Kate to slip in and snatch her sister's beau. Perhaps she used more outright tactics and did some bemusing herself, whereupon Eleanor married John Alonzo on the rebound. Now Kate would never have been swept off her feet by John Alonzo. His good looks, his good clothes, his charming ways would not have won her and she never in the world would have put up with his neglect.

Kate was a woman born at the wrong time. This was the Victorian era when a woman was expected to be merely an adjunct to a man, with her only field of endeavor home and children and making her man comfortable. This was not for her. She should have been born either five hundred years earlier, when she could have been chatelaine of a castle and managed her lord's lands when he was off on Crusade, or she should have been born into this day and age when she could have been a career woman. As it was, she managed the family—nearly to death—and was president of every ladies' club in town. She was always busy with "good works."

With all this surplus energy to channel, she was a natural for all the food and eating fads of the day, and when Aunty Kate took up a fad the whole household had to take it up. I remember when she embraced Fletcherizing—for the whole family. This was a simple way to good health that entailed the chewing of each mouthful of food one hundred times. This made for long, slow, silent meals as we all sat there counting. One hundred chews might be a fine idea for a piece of tough steak but it was hard to keep a bite of bread going that long. I remember another Fletcherizer who kept his count by the clicking of his jaws. This meant that everyone else had to synchronize with him or get hopelessly muddled in their count. There was a time when everyone had to chew gum for a specified length of time after each meal. This was doled out and everybody sat solemnly chewing the cud till Aunty Kate called time and the gum was ejected. I didn't mind—I liked to chew gum. She visited us once when carrots were the big thing. A large carrot was laid on a plate and set in front of her at each meal. This she ate with a crunching relish down to the last nibble. Since she had projecting front teeth and looked a bit like a rabbit herself, this charmed us kids.

Uncle Will Pierce was a dear. He had a silky beard, a sweet smile, and gentle ways. I think I felt in my youth that Uncle Will was hen-pecked and was pushed around like the rest of the family, but as I look back now, I doubt that he was. I think he was the head of his household and knew it. He just accepted Kate as she was and let her blow off that head of frustrated executive steam as she wished.

Honeymoon portrait of Edith Loring Jones Fullerton

Mother attended the Jenkintown Girls School and later went to Pratt Institute in Brooklyn where she was trained as a kindergarten teacher. Of course she learned homemaking skills at home. She sewed exquisitely and could turn her pretty, graceful hands to any kind of handwork.

When Dad asked Mother to marry him, I know Aunty Kate and Uncle Will disapproved entirely. Dad was nineteen years older than Mother and had led an adventurous life, and this probably tagged him as an "adventurer." I am sure these good Pennsylvania Quakers found him utterly alien, but his powers of persuasion did not fail him, and marry her he did.

They were married at Willowmere, and of course Dad saw to it that there were pictures of the whole thing. The decorations consisted of daisies and a certain delicate grass. The young ladies made daisy chains that festooned the porch. Mother carried white roses, I believe, but it was daisies that we hunted each June third for their wedding anniversary. It was always a bit of a challenge. In an early season we could find them, in a late year we might have to settle for a few buds showing white, but daisies and grasses we would have.

Dad designed the wedding dress and Mother made it. It was a completely simple Grecian gown with a heavy silk cord carried to the back from a knot at the neck and then back around the waist to tie and fall to the floor. It was a heavy, cream-colored silk and the simplicity was all on the outside. Inside, it was a contraption of body armor with whalebone stays and a million hooks and eyes. My sister Hope and I both were married in it. My eldest vetoed it for her wartime wedding, and eventually it fell into rags and ribbons as silk will. I burned it as one would burn the flag—why keep shreds and tatters. I still have the wedding veil.

Dad's position with the railroad gave him some interesting prerogatives and he arranged for a fast train to stop at Bristol to pick up the bridal pair when they set out on their honeymoon. Unfortunately, they boarded the train at one end and their car was at the other end, so, perforce, they made a triumphal march through car after car. Obviously bride and groom, they were the center of attention. Dad must have loved this and put on a most bridegroomly air, but Mother must have cringed. She was to learn that being married to Hal Fullerton meant being in the limelight, and she came to accept it—not happily but graciously.

Hal and Edith set up a home in Brooklyn and it was there that Hope was born, on June 10, 1899. There are many photographs of the baby with "Nursie" Mangan. This was Elizabeth Mangan, R.N., as Irish as a shamrock. She did private nursing, mostly baby cases. In those days, babies were born at home with a nurse to care for mother and baby. Nursie Mangan officiated at the births of all three of us, and in the course of time she saw my firstborn into the world.

The attending doctor was Frances Peele Beebe, my mother's doctor and friend for many years. Aunty Doctor was an oddity for her time. A woman had to be an oddity to study and practice medicine in the late 19th century. She was stepping into a man's world and her way was not made easy for her. Her sister was also a doctor and they had a niece who was a dentist. A family of rugged individualists.

Although Brooklyn was definitely included as part of the Blessed Isle, the Fullertons decided to move out into the country where they could have a house, not an apartment, and where there would be room for flower gardens, trees and lawns. So they moved out to Hollis and that is where I was born, at 11:58 p.m. on February 10, 1902, while an ice storm raged outside. Nursie Mangan officiated and the next morning Dad took a picture of a pot of daffodils blooming in the window.

ELF in her wedding dress, 1898

Childhood Days at Mira Flores

The Hollis interlude didn't last long. When I was six months old, we moved to Huntington. The house is still there and very little changed. It is on East Main Street, the second house from Spring Street on the south side. An old magazine article has a picture of the house when Dad and Mother bought it. It must have called for a lot of remodeling and "doing up." The grounds look to have been pretty much abandoned but they made a beautiful place of it. Dad named it Mira Flores, and I am sure the name came first but it was certainly followed in due time by a wealth of flowers.

Of the early days in Huntington of course I remember nothing. My first— my very first memory of anything—is of standing in a flower bed outside the French windows of the parlor on an early day in spring. The violets were in bloom—those dainty little English sweet violets that are white in the shade and flushed with lavender in the sun—and I was utterly happy in that aura of spring sun and growing things and violet fragrance. I have planted these violets in every garden I have had since then.

This bit of sun-warmed wall at my back and the newly released fragrance of plants growing around me was always a joy. I well remember looking for the same thing at Medford some years later. I used to climb out the dining room window and there, at the angle of the house wall and the glassed-in porch, I found a sun pocket where I could feel the warmth at my back and smell the growing things, including my violets.

We left Huntington when I was eight, so my memory pictures of the place are those of a four- or six- or eight-year-old child. To me it was all the world I needed. The back yard was of endless interest. There was a huge grapevine trained over a trellis attached to the back of the house. This area was paved with brick, the kitchen

HBF and Eleanor, 1902

door opened onto it and there was a long table where fruits and vegetables were prepared for cooking or canning. Then there was a long, long arbor, also covered by grapevines, which bisected the whole yard and led to the back gate and Platt Street. This grape arbor was enormous to my infant eyes—it stretched to infinity and to walk its length was an expedition.

On one side was the garden. I don't remember that too well except the years when Mother had the whole area in sweet peas. She was testing new varieties for Burpee and the lovely things grew on chicken wire stretched between posts, row on row of them. The picking must have been a job. They stood in great crocks on the back porch and many went to a very swanky restaurant somewhere down on the Sound—Bustanoby's Café and Chateau des Beaux Arts.

There were fat velvety pansies along the arbor—those black ones that held memories of Mexico days for Dad and Mother. There were tufted pansies too— the Scotch violas that refuse to grow for me now. There were fruit trees and vegetables. There was a big old apple tree at the corner of the house, close to the spot where I first remember smelling violets and spring, and we had a hammock there and a swing. An apple tree is a fine thing for children.

In front of the house a brick path led to the front gate. I remember peonies along this path and a sweet shrub (*Calycanthus*) growing nearby. We picked one of the strange red-brown blossoms each morning and tied it in the corner of a handkerchief. It was very comforting to sniff it all day at school.

There was also a huge horse chestnut tree near the house, and here Dad had erected the whalebone seat. This was an invention of his own, a one-of-a-kind. He had gotten a skeleton out at Bridgehampton when offshore whaling was still bringing in the occasional whale. This seat was about five feet long. Two fin bones made the arms at each end, and ten rib bones were fastened to a framework so that the concave surfaces made seat and back. Vertebrae made footstools. It was indeed a conversation piece, but I can't remember anyone sitting on it for any length of time. This was transferred to Medford when we moved there in 1910, but in altered and somewhat diminished form as even whale bones give up to weather in time.

Behind the horse chestnut and at the kitchen corner of the house was the summer house. This was referred to as the bower in an article written about the building of it, but I never heard it called anything but the summer house. It was an ultra-casual bit of construction, built of cedar poles with small cedars tossed on top as a semi-thatched roof. I think it was intended to be a gracious spot for serving tea on a summer afternoon, but I don't remember it ever being used much. As I recall, it was pretty spidery and damp and very close to the lake.

Ah—the lake! There is another article describing the construction of Mira Flores Lake. These articles appeared in *Country Life in America*, a rather posh magazine for the country gentleman published by Doubleday, Page and Company. I know the term "lake" is a relative one, and I think "pond" might have been more descriptive. However, I am sure Dad felt that Mira Flores Lake sounded better, and when Loring was born it became Lake Loring, a nice piece of alliteration.

Eleanor among the violets, Huntington, c.1906

"Mrs. Fullerton among the sweet peas." Huntington, c.1906

Mira Flores and Lake Loring. Hope is on the Japanese half-moon bridge to Pussy Willow Island.

Mira Flores Lake was originally known as Sheepwash Bog. There was a chain of ponds south of our place—three, I think, along Spring Street. An enchanting little brook came down from the ponds, gurgled under the road, and emptied into the bog. There was a little dam at the lower end and falls that carried the water on down a stream full of watercress, under Main Street and on north to a gorgeous swampy area full of anemones, tall grasses, small garter snakes, and all kinds of flora and fauna. Dad took us across now and then but it was far too much of a jungle for private exploration. An apartment house now rests on top of this primeval swamp.

Dad transformed the bog into a lake with an island in the middle, mostly by rebuilding the little dam. He loved a challenge like this. He added three bridges and stepping stones to the island. Down by the summer house he built a rustic cedar bridge that spanned the little dam and the falls. The second bridge was a Japanese half-moon bridge that connected the mainland with Pussy Willow Island.

We had an Indian wigwam on the island. Mother made Indian-style dresses, complete with red fringe, for Hope and me and our playmate Jeanette Duplay. We lived a very primitive life over there between dinner and supper. The handiest access to the wigwam was across the stepping stones. Hope and Jeanette bounded gaily back and forth but I was always timid as a rabbit and as clumsy and awkward as it is possible for a human to be, so I invariably fell off the stepping stones and ended up in tears and wet feet.

The Fullertons on the whalebone seat, Huntington, 1908

The third bridge, on the other side of the island, was also a challenge for me. At some point in the proceedings, Dad had a big locust tree cut down and split. One half was floated down to make a floor for the cedar bridge. Hope courageously rode this down the pond. The second half of the tree was thrown across between island and mainland on the east side. For some reason Dad saw fit to put it rounded side up. I suppose he liked the looks of the bark, or he may have felt the split side was too full of splinters.

This was another trial for me. The others would take a careless run, a few quick steps on the log, and they were across, but I would stand and agonize, finally screw up courage to dare all, and stagger across. I never fell in, but I don't know why.

We skated on the lake in the winter. Skates in those days were simply blades that clamped to the soles of our high-button shoes. Needless to say, we never became accomplished skaters. Dad attached sled runners to the wheels of Loring's carriage so we could push him across the ice.

A small area of the pond adjacent to the island was fenced in for the ducks so they would not foul the whole pond. Ducks are dirty things but they were mine and I loved them dearly. They were White Pekins. The drake wore a magnificent, feathery topknot on the side of his head. He was known as Mr. Drake Puddleduck and he had the same lordly air as the ducks in Beatrix Potter's Tom Kitten book. His ladies were named Rebeccah and Jemima from the same book and one had the interesting habit of laying her eggs in the water. I spent a good deal of time fishing them out with a rake. Dad liked duck eggs as did Jeanette's father.

The ducks nested on their own each spring so we had small ducks around. There was often one in the kitchen being brought up by hand for some reason. A scampery small duck can't have made housework easier. The ducks lived with the chickens in the chicken yard, which I always considered a fusty, dusty place and their house even fustier and dustier. I never could work up any enthusiasm for chickens.

Behind the chicken house grew lily-of-the-valley, and forget-me-nots flourished along the edge of the pond. This was Mother's favorite combination of flowers and I can still remember the day my brother Loring was born, when we went out and picked her a bouquet of lily-of-the-valley and forget-me-nots.

There was a little red barn next to the chicken house. When Dad's correspondence became too much to handle, he turned the top floor of the barn into an office and Miss Harriet Lee came to be his secretary. She was followed by Elliot Morton. He came from elsewhere—the friend of a friend or something—but he became a good Huntingtonian and married a Huntington girl.

And this brings us all the way around the demesne and to that back gate at the end of the arbor. This opened onto Platt Street, a quiet little street that still looks exactly as it did in 1910, with the big back yards of the Main Street houses on one side and smaller houses, quite unchanged, on the other.

Eleanor, Hope and ELF in the dining room at Huntington, c.1905

"Mira Flores. Oldest section of house, once the kitchen, used as den. Fireplace made serviceable and faced with field stone. Original crane, tea kettle, etc."

Right across from our back gate lived the Duplays. They moved there after we did but it can't have been long before we discovered Jeanette. She spent as much time at our house as we did and we spent as much time at hers as she. She had a dear little father, a little mother who was so good to us, a tiny grandmother who made fabulous currant bread, and a tall, rangy Aunt Dudie. I don't know how they all put up with us underfoot so much of the time but we always felt perfectly welcome and perfectly at home.

Jeanette was nearer Hope's age than mine and they spent a good deal of time together, but there were times when we all three played together, and sometimes Jeanette and I got out the dolls or paper dolls and Hope went off to do something less feminine. Hope and Jeanette went off at times and forgathered with Helen Wicks or Althea Ketcham or Eleanor Grumman. Eleanor's brother Roy was one of the early fliers and later started the Grumman aircraft company.

My extra playmate was George Funnell who lived in the third house up the street from us. He was a very unboylike boy who liked to play house and read books—we shared the Sunbonnet Sue books—and he grew up to be a bachelor professor of French at Amherst. His family made me feel at home too. There was his father, who worked in the Bank of Huntington, his tall, thin mother and his tall, thin sister Sarah—much older—and his little aunt, Miss Emily Banks.

Everyone was nice to children in those days and this meant being kind and loving and leaving us alone. We were never entertained. We made our own entertainments. We had a minimum of toys but plenty of room to play with them and we had peace and quiet in which to use our imaginations. We could have tremendous fun chopping up burdock stalks, cooking them in a doll's kettle over a doll's stone-cold stove and serving them as rhubarb to our appreciative dolls, properly dressed for the occasion. We spent hours watching the frogs around the lake, and when the tadpoles developed into frogs, the island was a hoppy hunting ground of tiny froglets that delighted us in their miniature perfection.

It takes very little imagination to take me back to the early years of the century when small town life was full of big lawns and gardens and duck ponds— much space and plenty of room and time. It was good for children to grow up at such an easy pace and in surroundings where they could find their own amusements, be free to roam, and get along with the business of growing up. It was a good age in which to be a child and a lovely setting for childhood.

When I hark back, it is sounds—sounds and smells—that shaped that world. Each sound had a chance to stand out, to make itself heard then. Now we live in such a maze of noise that you can't distinguish one sound from another and all the little ones are lost.

Let me shut that all out and think back to what I could hear on a summer day in Huntington in 1908. A lawnmower—hand-powered. A clinking, whirring sound accompanied by the lovely smell of new-mown grass.

A horse-drawn wagon in the street. That nice clop-clop that the cupped hoof makes on a dirt road. Sometimes it was the water cart that came through sprinkling down the dust, and then you had that unique smell of wet dust. You could run behind the cart and catch some of the sprinkle. Or it was the ice wagon that stopped out in front. There was the "chink" as the tongs grabbed hold of a cake of ice, steps on the brick walk, and you knew the ice was sliding into the cool maw of the icebox. There could even be a sliver of ice to suck when the iceman came back, clucked to his horse and moved on to the next house. The icebox stood outside the kitchen door under that giant grapevine and I don't remember it being moved inside for the winter. Probably January cooled the milk with no assist from the iceman.

Some lovely sounds came from the kitchen. One of the kitchen sounds that I loved was that of the eggbeater. This meant either that cream was being whipped or that eggs were being fluffed up for some luscious dessert. The meat chopper was another. I can't say that I was that crazy about hash, but the thud of the curved blade in the wooden bowl always pleased me. It was a busy sound, a homey sound, a cozy sound.

Ice cream was made in the big old hand-cranked wooden freezer in the brick-paved area under the grapevine outside the kitchen. The sound of the ice cream freezer, or just the sound of ice being chopped and crushed, would bring us flying. That is a fine sound—the fast whir of the gears that gets slower and slower and deeper and deeper as the ice cream begins to freeze, and oh! that moment when the freezer is opened to "see how it is coming." Then a few more laborious turns and the dasher has to be extracted, thoroughly scraped—alas, always too thoroughly—and some lucky child allowed to lick it.

Even my children knew the excitement of making ice cream by hand and licking the dasher. But I suppose you can't take anything out of context, and the hand-cranked freezer sounds don't reach their full value without the clopping of horses' hooves, the distant whir of a lawnmower, and all the lovely quiet that surrounded those sounds.

Another sound long lost was that of a woman singing at her work. There was always singing in the kitchen—not TV or radio belting it out, but the quiet singing with which a woman kept herself company. There were the old-timers that were old-timers even then—"Down by the Old Mill Stream" and "Annie Laurie"—but there were popular tunes too that got around somehow without the benefit of the electronic age. "Take Me Out to the Ball Game" was a hot number in my youth. Mrs. Funnell's girl used to sing one that ended "...down where the morning glories twine." It must have been of the nostalgic genre. That is all I remember of it, and heaven knows why that much should have stuck.

Of course every boy whistled. Pushing the lawnmower, walking to the store, gathering eggs, or just sloshing through the mud at the edge of a friendly stream, he whistled. Again, he was keeping himself company. Girls whistled too, but my mother used to say, "Whistling girls and crowing hens always come to some bad end." It didn't really stop us and she really didn't care, but it was obvious that whistling was not considered ladylike.

We sang as a family, too, around the piano. Mother played enough for this. Dad would attempt any song in the book. I doubt that Dad had a real singing voice—none of us did—but he had enthusiasm. We went from "Juanita," dripping with sentiment, to Dad's favorite, "My Darling Clementine," and all the Stephen Fosters.

Dad was a real family man and devoted to us kids. He played with us, he took us with him anywhere he went if we wanted to go (and we always did), and he read to us. I have a vivid memory picture of Dad reading to us about Mowgli and the Banderlog one winter's evening in the parlor. We usually used the den but this was in the parlor, I know. We must have made penuche fudge that day too, for the taste of penuche is part of the picture. I was sitting in his lap—a not unusual perch for me—and the firelight and warmth added their own richness to the whole.

He loved to read the *Just So Stories* and did full dramatic justice to "The Sing-Song of Old Man Kangaroo," "How the Elephant Got His Trunk," and "How the Whale Got His Throat." I am sure my readings of these classics to my own children—and grandchildren—were patterned on his.

The parlor piano at Huntington

Sunday always brought Uncle Peanuts. This was Frank Zoellar, a carpenter and builder who did the remodeling work on the house and became a fast and firm family friend. He had also built the Duplay house. He was a bachelor—a crusty bachelor—who lived down on Wall Street in rooms over his workshop. He would arrive every Sunday afternoon, reeking of cigar smoke and with pockets full of peanuts for us, the Sunday paper under his arm, and a box of monkey candy. These were molasses kisses that were wrapped in yellow waxed paper and came in a yellow box with monkeys all over it. We would swarm over him and he would read the funnies to us endlessly—the Katzenjammer Kids, Happy Hooligan, Little Nemo and Buster Brown. They were no more intellectual than the comics of today and just as full of thrown bricks and scary wizards.

Uncle Peanuts had a horse named Nuisance whom he loved dearly without ever admitting it. Nuisance was most amiable and it was she who drew the wagon every Christmas when we went out to Dix Hills to get a pitch pine Christmas tree. I have a vague memory of one year when we huddled under the blankets in the back of the wagon all the long way home. This was the year the snow was wet and heavy and made balls under the horse's hooves so that we had to stop every so often while Uncle Peanuts and Dad dug the stuff out. But Nuisance was a patient soul and never complained.

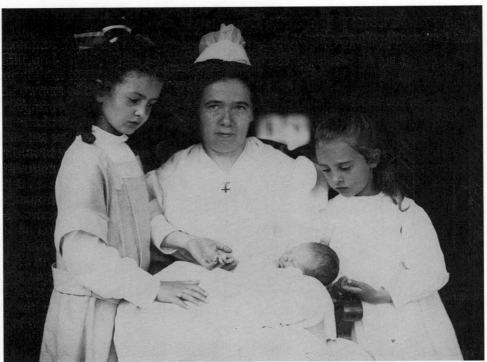

Nursie Mangan with Hope, Loring, and Eleanor, 1908

We had bread and molasses for Sunday night supper—dinner would have been an affair of roast beef and Yorkshire pudding—and this supper was good. I think it had been a treat for Dad in his young days for he harked back to the post-Civil War period when things were hard, and he still looked on bread and molasses as a treat for Sunday night.

I remember the Sunday sessions with Uncle Peanuts and the funnies as being in the den. This room was just in front of the dining room and there is a picture of it in *How to Make a Vegetable Garden*, one of my mother's books. The den had a huge fireplace made of rugged rocks and boasted an overpowering decor. Dad liked to have his mementos around him, so the Mexican serapes were tossed over chairs, his spurs hung by the fireplace, his Mexican hat was on the mantel, and pictures were everywhere.

It was the Victorian era of overdecoration anyway, but what a job it must have been to keep it all clean. We had a maid. Everyone on Main Street had a maid. Nearly all of them were Irish girls fairly fresh from County Cork. Our maid was Nettie O'Connell and she was with us for a long time. She and Mother did the work of the house and it was real manual labor. We did have plumbing but the kitchen stove burned coal and the lights were oil lamps. Brooms and mops and dusters did the cleaning, and the laundry was done on scrubbing boards in washtubs. Damp tea leaves sprinkled on the rug before sweeping it kept the dust down a little. And twice a year the rugs went out to hang on the clothesline where they were beaten clean with the carpet beater. No wonder woman's work was never done.

Upstairs there were four bedrooms. Dad's and Mother's room was at the front and a nice little room next to it was mine until Loring came along. Behind their room was the guest room that was used by Grandma Busy, Dad's stepmother, when she came to visit us. It was here that she and Mother sat and visited and sewed and read aloud, and I must have been one of the party a good deal of the time for I remember it very plainly.

Two steps down and over the kitchen were the bathroom and Hope's and my room. When the folks bought the house they had a dormer put into the roof to make this room. We also used it as our playroom, and doll gear and music box and rocking horse are part of my memories.

I can well remember lying in my bed and looking out one or another of the windows. The one in front was high but I could look out into a cherry tree that grew close to the house. In the leafless branches in winter I found patterns that became very much mine. One was of a baby chick that I can still see. And when spring came and the cherry tree bloomed I could watch it each morning as it progressed from fat buds to full-blown, snow-white flowers. And that's when the orioles came to add their golden beauty and their golden song.

The other window was at the low end of the room—a small window close to the floor. Through this I could see the summer house and in June this was covered with a little golden rambler rose. I must have been an early waker for I remember lying there and reveling in the beauty of these yellow roses in all their early morning goldenness before the sun faded them out to plain yellow. So many of my memories are pictures like this accompanied by surges of feeling—and so many of them connected with growing things. I was fortunate to live in such an environment.

Loring was born when I was six, on May 24, 1908. Nursie Mangan came some time ahead of the event so I trotted along while she and Mother walked around the gardens or worked on baby garments and all the other necessaries.

This must have been when Nursie Mangan took us to church with her and I was introduced to Catholic symbols and rituals. I found it merely interesting, just as I viewed the doings in the Episcopal church where we went with Jeanette. We had no church training ourselves. Apparently Dad and Mother felt no need to affiliate with any church although, if we had lived longer in Huntington, it might have come into the picture. Mother had been reared by Quakers, than whom nobody could have less ritual. Dad's religious background, except for all those baptisms and the reading of the Bible to his grandfather, was minimal, although he once wrote, "I was firmly founded in the Episcopal, Shouting Methodist, and Unitarian faiths...strong but widely differing types yet founded on the Golden Rule." And the Golden Rule was indeed his foremost guiding principle.

Rogue in the goat harness, pulling Loring, and Eleanor, 1909

So Loring was born, the pride and joy of one and all—the son and heir for Dad, and the Crown Prince for the rest of us. He grew to be a golden-haired, blue-eyed charmer and we all loved him. Jeanette was one of his court and George Haggerty was his loyal attendant. George was our handyman. He mowed lawns, brought up the coal for the kitchen stove, took out the ashes, and fed the chickens. He took special delight in taking Loring out in his carriage. Here he had a partner in Rogue, our lovely dog.

Rogue was a golden collie of the border collie type. He was that dog in a thousand that you never forget, a perfect gentleman who fitted into the household as one of the family. One of his great pleasures was to assist George in the daily stroll with the baby carriage. George harnessed him to the front of the carriage and away they went. This harness calls for an explanation. It was in truth a goat harness. It was rather smart in those days for the children of the wealthy to have a small wagon drawn by a goat. I think you will still find the occasional photograph, among early archives of the great, with the son of the illustrious Mr. and Mrs. So-and-So driving on the estate in his goat cart.

Well, we had wagon, goat, and harness, not because we were scions of wealth but because the goats were raised on the Experimental Farm of the Norfolk and Western Railroad in Roanoke, Virginia. In his position as Director of Agriculture for the LIRR, Dad had become good friends with the Director of the Norfolk and Western farm. I know Hope and I once went with him on a trip down there and we acquired a goat.

I don't think this lasted long. I don't know who fell heir to the goat but it was Rogue who inherited the harness and he wore it with pride. It must have been a pleasant sight on Main Street when a delighted George Haggerty, a dignified Rogue, and a perfectly placid Loring went out for an airing.

I started school in Huntington and got as far as the third grade there. I well remember the episode of my cut hair when I was in kindergarten. Hope came by a pair of shears and undertook to do my hair over. Mother came home from calling on some lady of her acquaintance, took one look at my mangled head, and burst into tears. I don't know what befell Hope—a stern and lengthy lecture from Dad, I imagine—but I was taken to the barber and my head was shaved. She must have really cut me to the quick. The next day Mother went with me to kindergarten to see me through my debut as a baldy. It seems to have taken ages for it to grow out for the pictures go on and on of Eleanor with little or no hair.

Eleanor and Hope after the haircut, 1907

ELF, HBF, Eleanor with shaven head, and Uncle Peanuts in the den at Huntington, 1907

Peace and Plenty, the Farm at Wading River

Dad had decided that the way to bring people to Long Island and the way to prove the wonders of the Blessed Isle was to prove that it was an agricultural paradise—or could be made into one. So in 1905 the railroad succumbed to his clamors and agreed to start an Experimental Station.

The Island had miles and miles of scrub oak waste, the result of the timber cutting of generations. Lumber had gone to the west end to build the city and more wood had gone as fuel for the wood fires. Finally, they were hauling wood for the copper smelters in Long Island City.

This went on even into our days at Middle Island in the 1920s. Grandma Bayles, our next door neighbor there, was from Miller Place and she used to tell of the days when lumbering was the big winter occupation. In the summer, the sloops would come in to the North Shore on the high tide and the word went around. When the tide went out the ships would be grounded. Then the horse-drawn wagons splashed out and the timber was heaved aboard. On the next high tide, the sloops floated again and went their way to the city.

This cut-over scrub land lay idle but Dad said it could be cleared to raise profitable crops—profitable for the farmer and profitable for the LIRR that would transport carloads of potatoes and cauliflower, eggs and lima beans to the New York markets, as well as carloads of farm equipment and Maine seed potatoes to the farmers. The wiseacres said the land was no good, which was all Dad needed. He rose to the bait like a hungry perch and, with the blessing of the LIRR and the treasury of the parent Pennsylvania Railroad, he took off. Like a rocket!

In 1905 the railroad bought ten acres at Wading River for $23 an acre and Experimental Station Number One was born. My mother told the whole story of developing the farm, which they named Peace and Plenty, in one of her books, *The Lure of the Land*. She told how Dad ignored all the accepted and slow ways of

"The Junior Partner blowing stumps by battery." Wading River, 1905   *Courtesy of Suffolk County Historical Society*

carving a farm out of the wilderness. He used his ingenuity, the assorted knowledge he had come by in his years at various jobs in various parts of the country, and his terrific drive. He got things done because he pitched in and worked himself, he listened to advice and used it if it was good, or he invented ways and means to do things and cared not how unorthodox they were. He had only one objective—to prove that the "no-good" acres of Long Island could blossom like the rose, and a whole lot faster.

In one of his earlier jobs he had made the acquaintance of dynamite. He certainly used it to good effect in clearing land quickly for the farm. A fruit tree planted in a dynamite-dug hole made two years' growth in one, the result of thoroughly pulverized soil and a fine inoculation of nitrogen.

I don't remember the clearing days for we were in Huntington and Dad and Mother went back and forth. Dynamiter Charles Kissam of Huntington was engaged to do the blasting. The work force was a crew of Italians, mostly immigrants newly arrived in the Land of Opportunity. Dad used sign language and demonstrated how he wanted things done, and he was quite likely to fling his Mexican Spanish at them. They would reply with an assortment of Italian dialects, and the foreman, Lorenzo Balzarano, would straighten them out.

Mike Cooper (Miguel Coperillo), who was farm foreman when the time came for plowing and planting, was one who had been here long enough to learn English. Mike stayed at the farm until it was sold in 1913. Then he went into the market garden business in Wading River, and if I know my Dad he saw to it that Mike was well established.

The men lived in a retired freight car, built their own bunks and comforts, and fed themselves. Water had to be brought from the Wading River station and two water boys trudged the mile and a half each way with pails of water. In time, Dad had a well driven, a kerosene engine installed, and a water tower erected with a 5000-gallon water tank, and then water flowed all over the farm. This water tower survived for decades despite the changes in the surrounding area, and I would see it when I passed and remember the summer of 1906 when we lived on the Farm.

This was the year that the Exposition Internationale at Milan awarded the farm a bronze medal for Dad's "rapid, cheap and common-sense method of clearing undeveloped territory" by using dynamite. According to the *Long Island Agronomist*, this was an exposition that "brought together all manner of devices for the improvement and safety of mankind." The *Agronomist* was a small monthly publication that Dad wrote and he and Mother put together after they had established the LIRR's second farm at Medford in 1907. It was intended to keep the world informed on the progress of the two farms, and on agriculture in general.

During the Wading River farm's first year, Dad had to commute from Huntington—by train. How else? But once things were really moving, he needed to be on the spot. So by early summer in 1906 a portable house was up, water was available, and it was feasible to move the family out.

Recent immigrants from Italy clearing land for the farm at Wading River, 1905

Mike Cooper scything, 1906

I was only four years old so my memories of that summer in Wading River are fragile and fleeting. I liked it—I guess I was happy anywhere—except for the trains. The track was very close to the house and the roadbed was raised a bit at this point so the trains really thundered by. There was a wire fence along the front, and a gate where the trains would stop on request. After all, the farm was part of the railroad. So it was all right when a train came to a puffing halt, but when they highballed right through I was terrified. At the first sound of a train in the distance I took to the recesses of the house. I well remember one day when I decided I would not run and I stayed on the porch as the monster drew nearer and nearer. At the last moment—too late to escape—I buried my head in my hands and just hoped I would survive. Obviously I did.

The horse barn was part retired freight car and part rather informal construction. The packing shed was just a tarpaper-covered roof thrown out from this barn with tables underneath. Here the vegetables were washed and packed for shipment in Home Hampers, an enterprise that will be explained later. We liked to climb up on this roof for there were drops of tar along the seams that we could pick off and chew. We would also climb into the hay mow and toss hay down into the mangers for the two big horses, Texas and Buckeye. They were amiable souls.

They had been Railway Express horses and had hauled express wagons around the city so I don't know how good they were as plow horses. The Express company belonged to the LIRR too. The chicken house was another freight car, which seemed satisfactory to all chickens. There was a greengage plum tree in the chicken yard.

There were pigs. Elihu Miller of Wading River sold Dad four piglets and they lived in a pigpen at the south end of the barn. We each adopted one and were permitted to name him. Hope coyly named hers Rosebud, I chose Violet, Mother graciously named hers Elihu, but Dad opted for Eventually. A most suggestive name and not one to gladden the heart of a young porker, but I thought it a fine name. I called him Evench Willy.

Of course there were flowers. Both Dad and Mother loved them, and one of Dad's most unorthodox ideas was that a farm homestead should be attractive and this one must be dressed up the very first season. So quick-growing vines—morning glories and wild cucumber—grew on fences, ferns made shady spots green, and annuals bloomed around the house. Even a pile of roots that had been blown clean by the dynamite but had not been cleared away became a riot of color with climbing nasturtiums planted around it.

Dad invented a birdbath that stood beside the flagpole (there was always a flagpole with the flag flying). This was the first of many similar birdbaths. It was

"Peace and Plenty Cottage. The Homestead at No. 1 in the summer of 1906." At right is the base of the water tower with outdoor wash stand and indoor bathroom.

"Prize winners—a few squash and some pumpkins." HBF with Hope, Loring and
Eleanor, 1908

made of a stump. Any stump with a hollow center would do—rightside-up or
upside-down, it didn't matter. A little cement might be needed to make it
watertight, then a very small pipe was worked through a convenient root or up
through the base, and a gas jet was fastened to the top. This was the kind of gas
jet used for lighting, not cooking. It took very little water and the gas jet made for
a fine spray that delighted the birds. The running water was always cold and clean
and a few rocks or some gravel made a catch basin and a second pool nearby. I have
always wanted to make one again, but where would one find a gas jet these days?

I made the acquaintance of whip-poor-wills at Wading River. There must
have been hundreds of them and they were deafening around the cottage but I slept
well in spite of them. The quail called back and forth all day and they must have
been delighted with the grain plantings.

Dad sprained his knee that summer and had trouble with it from then on. It
didn't slow him down—he just stormed around on crutches. Perhaps if he had
favored it for a few weeks it might not have been unreliable the rest of his life.
Crutch or not, he set off a fabulous bunch of fireworks on the Fourth of July, to
our great delight.

On August 7, Dad and Mother invited a dozen gentlemen of the press to
dinner. Eleven months and a day earlier, these same men, editors of newspapers

and magazines from New York and Brooklyn, had been invited to watch the first stumps being dynamited. They had been very skeptical about the whole project and were sure it was a waste of time and money. Now they were sitting on a green lawn, surrounded by flowers and thriving fields, eating a "boiled dinner scrub-oak style" that featured corned beef and ten different vegetables grown on land they had predicted to be worthless. Dad designed the menu and embellished it with drawings of everything from flying stumps to caterpillars. After a tour of the farm, they left totally convinced.

When fall came we went back to Huntington. The cat had to be retrieved from the woods first. This was Biskie, our big old Manx cat who felt about trains in the front yard the same way I did. He left for the woods as soon as we arrived. He did come in every evening with a contribution for Dad—a mouse or a chipmunk—and after a short conversation he would return to the woods. For a much-pampered cat who had never known anything wilder than Lake Loring he became very self-sufficient in this pioneering environment.

The menu designed by HBF for the dinner served to members of the press 11 months after the first blasting at Wading River, 1906

Prosperity Farm at Medford

When Dad had proved that the North Shore could blossom like the rose, the cry went up that he had good soil there but that the middle of the Island—that land of pitch pine, scrub oak and sandy soil—was useless. To Dad there was not an inch of the Blessed Isle that wasn't pure gold, so he persuaded LIRR President Ralph Peters to sanction a second farm.

Both Dad and Mother felt that Long Island farmers and their wives could benefit tremendously from all the scientific know-how and the new ways of doing things that the schools of agriculture and home economics at Cornell were pouring out, and this was another reason Dad felt they must have the second farm—to *show* the local farmers that it paid to irrigate or improve your stock or better the working conditions for your help or even for your wife.

Armed with a list of available land, Dad and Mr. Peters boarded a train and went to look for a site. East of Medford, an eighty-acre parcel was pointed out from the train window. It looked like the perfect challenge, it was right along the railroad, and the price was right. The railroad bought this tract in 1907 for $15 per acre, and LIRR Experimental Station Number Two (later called the Demonstration Farm) was under way. It was named Prosperity Farm.

How on earth Dad managed one farm at Wading River and one at Medford while living in Huntington I don't know. He traveled, as I said, by train. To Wading River this was feasible, for they were on the same line, but Medford was on the Main Line. He would have had to go to Hicksville where the two lines met and then out to Medford. But he managed it and I remember his going and coming. He often brought me flowers from Medford—rabbit's foot clover, wild pea (that pink and yellow one that only grows in the middle of the island) and lupine.

The trolley ran from Huntington Harbor (Halesite) to the station in those days and we would walk up to New York Avenue to meet Dad when he came home.

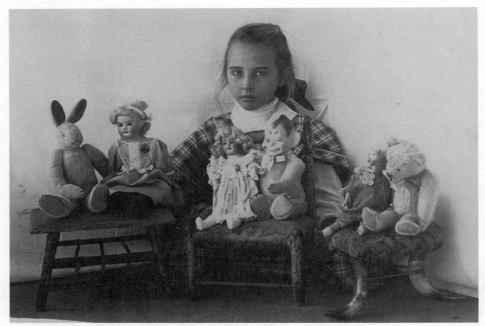

Eleanor with her dolls. Billiken is third from right. c.1909

He would stop with us to look at the huge fire horses in the fire house on Main Street, or stop to talk to someone even though he knew supper was waiting. Dad was always stopping to talk to someone.

One evening we stopped at a gift shop and he bought me a Billiken, to my astonished delight. This Billiken was like a white teddy bear with a composition face wearing a gleeful smile. I had been admiring this individual in the store window for some time and Dad somehow knew. I doubt that I said anything—I was not one to ask for things. Maybe he saw my longing, maybe the amusing face appealed to him too. Anyway, he bought it and I carried it home with great joy. It was one of my treasures for a long time. Dad was always doing things like this. He loved to give, and I am sure he knew I appreciated both his giving and his love behind it.

We spent two summers at Prosperity Farm before we moved there permanently in 1910. Those two summers are a bit of a blur to me. Again we lived in a portable house—we eventually had six of these portables on the Farm—and we watched all the buildings going up. I use the capital F advisedly. It was always called the Farm and was so known at least all over Medford. You got the mail for the Farm, we lived at the Farm, a man worked at the Farm. It was rather like an Englishman referring to the Manor.

It must have been a huge job setting up the Farm and planning the layout. The buildings stretched the whole width of the acreage in order to show all to those who passed on the trains. Uncle Peanuts had the contract for putting up the Farm buildings and he moved out from Huntington with his crew of carpenters and painters. They built a shack beside the Farm railroad siding and we used to visit them there. They had a cook, as did every work gang in those days, an older man called Cappy. Of the carpenters I remember only one, a long, lean Yankee type known as Skinny.

Many of the buildings are still standing. When Uncle Peanuts built, he built for the ages. I'll bet the Homestead was as sound as the proverbial dollar until it was razed by a fire in 1977.

After we moved into the Homestead, the original portable house was dubbed the Postscript and was used to accommodate the many apprentices and students who later came to the Farm for short-term learning jobs.

The Homestead was the heart of the complex, the volcanic crater where Dad planned and plotted what to do next to astonish the world, where he sat for hours inventing ways to do it, and from which he erupted to direct, supervise, pitch in, or just encourage with his endless vitality and enthusiasm. The Homestead was to be a model farmhouse, for Dad was a revolutionary in thinking that the farm home and the farm wife should have as much consideration as the cow barn and the cows. In Upstate New York and through New England you can still see the old-style farm with fine big barns and a bedraggled little house where convenience and beauty were completely ignored.

Dad also had another consideration. This was the LIRR Farm and as such would be open to the public. In fact, the public would be lured in any way Dad could contrive. To see was to believe and he wanted all the world to see what could be done with his Blessed Isle.

People who came by regular train—and how else?—perforce had to spend the day. The morning train came in from the west at ten a.m. and the afternoon train returned at four p.m. Sometimes people would write ahead and were expected, but quite often the train just stopped at the Farm and disgorged entirely unexpected visitors. This never bothered Dad. He would stop what he was doing and talk happily straight through to four o'clock, or keep on working if it was that kind of job and still talk straight through to four. But Mother *had* to stop what she was doing and be present. Dad always wanted her to be a part of everything. And she also had to conjure up lunch. So the house had to be adequate for serving punch and cookies to a trainload of newspapermen or entertaining a delegation from the Agricultural Commission of Peru for a whole day.

The first requirement of any living place is water, and on a farm especially, but on a farm such as Dad created, oceans of water were needed. Besides us in the Homestead, there were eventually four families living on the Farm, there was all the stock—horses, cows, chickens and pigs—and besides that, Dad laid out overhead irrigation on the big market garden field. This was an innovation and a bit of a contradiction for him. One of his great selling points for the Blessed Isle was that we never had a drought. Point number two was that, should the gentle rains from Heaven fail, the heavy dews of summer nights would supply moisture.

He took many a picture of a dew-drenched cabbage to prove this. However, he installed a Skinner irrigation system—overhead pipes that swung back and forth—and it was well used.

So his first major concern was water, and the well drillers moved in. They soon struck water but surface water would not do, so they went on down to second water and tapped, at 68 feet, the underground stream that is said to run under the whole Island. Once the water was an actuality and in the pipes, an enormous pumping system was set up. This was a matter of great oily black gears and things that made fearful noises. We stood in the doorway and watched with trepidation while Ted Tuddenham, or whoever was the current engineer, went around with a hunk of waste in hand and a knowledgeable look on his face. There was also a kerosene engine like the one that was used at Wading River. According to the *Agronomist*, it was a two-and-a-half-horsepower job.

There was of course a water tank—a wooden tank of five thousand gallon capacity erected high above the pump house so that gravity took the water where it was needed. Dad was never one to waste any useful space so he conceived an observation deck under the tank and over the roof of the pump house. With a good floor, waist-high railing, and four corner seats, it was a fine place for a panoramic view of the Farm.

It was a good spot to take the breeze on a summer's afternoon with a supply of plums or peaches or peas or carrots or whatever took our fancy at the moment. We kids made good use of it. Visitors were taken up there, if they could bear to walk through the murky engine regions to reach the stairs, and it made a good introduction to a tour of the Farm.

There was an iron ladder that led to a walkway around the base of the water tank itself. This was the spot I liked. I dearly loved ladders and would climb anywhere but we were not allowed to go to this height unless Dad went with us. It was from here, in 1919, that I saw the R34—a British dirigible, the first airship to cross the ocean. A strange sight, this fat gray sausage that had actually flown from Europe. The dawn of a whole new era indeed.

The observation deck was also a useful spot to keep fire watch during the spring and fall when the woods were dry and fire was a common menace. During forest fire season we never went anywhere without shovels in the car and we seldom got to Medford and back with the mail without taking time out for a small blaze along the track. Sometimes we had horrendous, racing fires when the flames went through the tops of the trees, leaped roads, and swept over acres of ground before they could be controlled.

There were no fire wardens in those days. It was every man for himself, and when smoke billowed, every man in the area dropped what he was doing and went to fight the fire. It might be five miles to the east today and no threat to us, but next week it could be in our own backyard. So everyone rallied. I remember one fire so close that the men had the hose on the chicken house. Dad and Mother were away,

The Postscript, where the family lived until the Homestead was completed

and whoever had charge of us kids was badly shaken. The horse was hitched to the buggy and we were taken to Medford for safekeeping.

Besides water in abundance, Dad decreed electricity for his model farm. We had to make our own "juice" so Dad and the Edison company put their collective heads together and came up with a system that would light the Farm. This was run by the same engine that ran the water pump but don't ask me how you "run" an electrical plant. I believe there was a large bank of storage batteries involved. The whole place was just a giant's machine shop to me.

We did have lights all over the Farm and this made for comfort, reduced fire hazards, and was a distinct innovation for farm life. That was the extent of electrification—lights. In this day, when even the can opener works by electricity, it may sound inadequate, but I don't think anyone suffered even if we did have to beat the eggs by hand, iron the clothes with a Mrs. Potts sadiron heated on a coal stove, provide a bit of extra heat with a smelly little kerosene stove, and run the sewing machine by woman-power.

We had central heating—a huge, fat furnace that sent hot air heat up to the registers throughout the house. You could stand on one of these registers and the hot air would balloon out your skirts and envelop you in warmth. The sound of Dad shaking down the furnace and adding coal was a most warming and cheery sound in itself on a cold morning. The coal came by the carload and was dumped by the siding to be hauled in the farm wagon to its various destinations. Each house had its coalbin for the cooking and heating stoves.

Prosperity Farm, c.1911.

The pump house was on one side of the Homestead and the horse barn on the other. I daresay Cornell would disapprove of living quarters and barn set as cozily as they were at Medford, but we found no fault with the barn next door. The side toward the house was a blank wall and all the horsey operations went on on the other side.

Our two work horses, Old Dominion, or Dom, and Pennsy, were veterans of Railway Express Company service and had been retired to the Farm. They were an ill-matched pair but the farm work did get done. We also had a saddle horse named Peg O' My Heart. We loved her dearly and visited her often, fed her carrots and apples and tasty tufts of new spring grass, but she was seldom ridden and she lived a delightful horse life in a sunny, comfortable stall with the top half of her door open to the world most of the time. We had a fine Western saddle but neither Hope nor I seemed to care much for riding her. We had no instruction. One just got on a horse and rode, according to Dad.

Behind the horse barn was the little feed house with zinc-lined feed bins which were very discouraging to the occasional mouse who tried for a free meal. Then there was the chicken house where Dad tried various breeds of chickens and learned to hate White Leghorns. Hope's bantams lived there and also my ducks. There were three handsome Black Minorca chickens named Ivanhoe, Rebecca and Rowena. Nothing went unnamed.

Mr. Drake Puddleduck and his harem had been moved from Huntington and a trio of mallards appeared. I was very fond of Tom Puddleduck and he lived to a ripe old age. He had two wives who consistently stole nests in odd places, once in the doghouse, but I doubt that the dog minded. He spent very little time there. A dog led a free and untrammeled life in those days on the Farm.

The machinery shed housed our first two cars, a Brush and an International Harvester IHC. The Model T that came later was a more elegant piece of machinery and required better housing so a garage was eventually built. This was made of tile and was rather ugly but Dad took care of that. He planted a Persian lilac. This was Mother's favorite. I didn't care for it then, but as the years have passed I have come to admire the reddish lilac color and the great ostrich plumes of the Persian. Both the garage and the lilac are still there.

Chiquita Casa, right behind the Homestead, was a little two-room affair where we girls were to learn the arts of housekeeping. There was a range in the kitchen, a set of dishes (with violets) and a set of cutlery. I still have one of the forks. It is the one that can really tell me when the baked potatoes are done. As it turned out, Chiquita Casa was mostly used as a schoolhouse. It was a pleasant place for school. There was a birch tree outside one window and a chokecherry outside another so there were always birds to watch and this lightened our lessons. A stump birdbath stood under the birch tree, an added attraction for the birds.

For four years Hope and I had a teacher of our own—called a governess but really just a teacher. This was not snobbishness, it was necessity. It must have been thought out before the folks ever decided to move away from Huntington and a good public school system. In 1910, the country schools were pretty impossible. We would have had to go to the West Yaphank school, some three miles back through the woods. This was the old-fashioned one-room school with just anybody for a teacher. The school board's only requirement was that a teacher should come cheap. A high school education was more than enough to qualify.

So that is why Dad and Mother engaged a teacher for us and established us in Chiquita Casa for regular school sessions. First we had Rachel Rikert, a nice farm girl from upstate. She was followed by Frances Campbell who was with us for two years. She lived with us, of course, and I think Mother enjoyed her company. She had no real training as a teacher. I think her family had "come down in the world." Her home was in Bay Ridge and she went home for weekends.

Miss Campbell was a pretty young woman with soft dark hair that she wore in the Charles Dana Gibson style. I used to love to watch her brush and comb it and put it up in the Psyche knot on top of her head, with neat little side combs holding the pompadour in place. By this time my Hope-shorn hair had grown out but I never achieved more than two very unimpressive mouse-colored braids which were usually tied with two very large bows.

Miss Campbell taught us music, I believe, and was certainly a good influence, culturally speaking. We acquired a player piano and a collection of music rolls intended to introduce us to "good music." We had such numbers as "Anitra's Dance," "Claire de Lune," the "Poet and Peasant Overture" and such. I enjoyed this a lot and felt that I played with deep understanding and proper rendition. I was very nimble with the levers that allowed you to shade the music. We never got as far as Bach, Beethoven and Brahms.

We also had an art teacher, Pearl Price. She was Canadian, a commercial artist who came out from New York once a week and tried to develop our artistic talents. I think Hope did fairly well but I was a total loss. I never could, and I can't to this day, draw anything. I struggled with daffodils, lady's slippers, still lifes and landscapes, and it was only Miss Price's few deft strokes that made them presentable. At coloring I was better—I was quite happy with color—but you have to outline something before you can color it. Miss Price eventually married Frank Keill, one of the office force, but our art careers came to an end before that.

After Frances Campbell came Miss Letitia Steelman. This is precisely the name Dickens would have given her if she had appeared in one of his books. She was the best teacher we had. I think she even had a college education and had been a teacher. She came to the Farm in this capacity because she wanted to learn about farming. Eventually she and a cousin bought a farm at the corner of the Medford-Port Jefferson road and Granny Road. Since they both came from Michigan, Dad named it "Wolverine Ranch," designed their letterhead, helped them with produce for the Home Hamper business that they tried to organize, and was their general mentor and teacher. They gave up after a short time and I don't know what became of them. We were not fond of Miss Steelman, although she tried her best to be likeable. She had a frightening smile—all huge white teeth—but we did learn a lot from her.

At the east end of the Farm stood the portable house occupied by the Newton family—Tom and his wife and two sons, Ed and Harry. Tom was the farm foreman, not an onerous job as Dad was the one who held the reins. The Newtons were English, from Suffolk I believe. I don't know what phase of farming had been Tom's in England but he was at home with all farm work. The cows were his special care. His slow, solid footsteps went by the house at bedtime as he went back to the cow barn to check his charges for the night, and they were even heard in the wee small hours if a cow was calving.

Tom was a stocky, calm, good-natured man who never changed his pace or his air of contentment with life. He was fond of us kids and never found us a nuisance. Loring admired him and liked to walk beside him imitating his slow, steady plowman's walk. I liked to watch him milk and I had many a cup of frothy, warm milk straight from the cow—unpasteurized, unhomogenized, even unstrained and, in the early days, from cows not even tuberculin tested, but gee! it was good.

Tom was a good man with horses too and he plowed a fine, deep, straight furrow. His son Harry was just like him and in time he plowed his furrow just as deep and straight. Ed had no flair for farming but he did have one for machinery.

Hope, Eleanor, Loring and teacher Rachel Rikert outside Chiquita Casa, the schoolroom

He went off to World war I, was in a machine gun outfit and was the only man from Medford to be killed in that war. The town planted a tree in his honor in front of the Grange Hall.

It was Tom Newton who suggested that Dad try broad beans, an English favorite. Dad was already getting much of his seed from England—from Carter and from Sutton—for the English are fussy about their varieties. Unfortunately, the English start out with the grandest vegetables in the world and then ruin them in the cooking, everything reduced to a pallid mush. The broad beans were a great success with the Newtons but nobody else ate them. They had beautiful and unusual black and white flowers which I admired.

Tom also had a great love for celery and never was celery so lovingly tended. The trenches were dug deep and manured with a lavish hand. It was well irrigated during the summer and fed by watering pot with liquid manure from the cow barn. In the fall it was hilled deeply to blanch to creamy crispness and finally what wasn't eaten before frost was transferred, roots and all, to the root cellar and replanted in damp, deep sand to be used during the winter.

Any fresh vegetable was welcome in January and February and a root cellar was a valuable thing to have. Lord knows it was a simple operation—merely a hole

Harry Newton riding Peg O' My Heart, 1915

dug in sandy soil and a peaked roof laid over the top of a minimum of framework. Racks with slatted or wire mesh bottoms held carrots, beets, cabbages, turnips and potatoes. The celery was in the sandy floor and Dad even treated endive or chicory the same way to blanch it. The place smelled grand—earthy and vegetably. I never minded being sent out for potatoes for supper, and there was always a carrot available for my rabbit or for Peg O' My Heart.

Of course not everything wanted this damp, cool treatment. Apples, squash, and pumpkins went into the house cellar which was dry but still had dark, cool corners for such storage. The onions were spread out on the attic floor and were very pungent all winter.

Part of the cellar had been made into a canning storage room. This was a good-sized room completely shut off from the main cellar. It had two windows for ventilation as needed and was lined all around with shelves. By the end of summer they were packed solid with the products of Mother's canning. From the first rhubarb and strawberries, through to the last peaches and the last planting of beans, Mother canned. A misnomer, for everything went into glass jars, and she early learned to use the cold pack method. Both Mother and Dad were constantly looking for newer and better ways of doing things and the Department of Home Economics at Cornell steered Mother in many "newfangled" ways like cold packing your tomatoes instead of using the open kettle method. Because of the word from Cornell that light would fade glass-packed fruits, she installed dark blue curtains all along the shelves of the canning cellar.

Mother made jams and jellies of all kinds, her piccalilli we loved, and one year she tried her hand at little sweet pickles. She achieved one crock that was superb. It stood on the floor under the bottom shelf. She covered the pickles with grape leaves and a plate, and put a flatiron on top to keep them submerged. However, it was no problem at all to lift iron, plate and grape leaves, reach in and extract a cold, crisp, sweetly sour little pickle—and then another. This crock was so successful—and so short-lived—that I think Mother gave up. Too few ever got to the table.

The barrels of apples were in the cellar too. Before our trees reached bearing age—a matter of five to seven years—Dad sent upstate for apples which arrived in barrels. We must have had Rhode Island Greenings, Baldwins and, definitely, Russets. I well remember how good they smelled and how good they tasted. Dad once got a keg of grapes too. They must have come from Spain for they were packed in shredded cork. Strange material to us, and the grapes strange too. A far cry from the fat Concords and Niagaras that made late summer a juicy joy, but we ate them with relish and probably left a trail of seeds behind us.

To return to the Newtons, Mrs. Newton was called Lady Newton by Dad and hence by the rest of us. I have no idea what her first name was. Dad had a thing about maintaining people's dignity. This was the day when servants were servants, with no bones about it, but Dad worked at building dignity and respect for everyone. Mrs. Newton sounded too formal but he felt she rated a title of some sort—very likely because of us kids. He was a fiend for nicknames anyway and, since she was English, she became Lady Newton. She was the Farm dairymaid and was on duty morning and evening to oversee the straining, separating, and setting of the cream, the bottling of milk for the farm families, and the meticulous washing up. I was her assistant and I was *usually* there to do the washing.

This dairy was again a pure invention of Dad's. Cleanliness and coolness were the necessities in dealing with milk, so the dairy—or milk house as it was also called—was dug like the root cellar out of the ground with only enough room above ground for many windows, which were screened. A deep sink was lined with zinc, and on a connecting counter was a pail rinser that Dad invented. A water pipe came through the counter and was topped with a "rose" or head from a watering pot. One turned a pail upside down over the rose, turned on the blazing hot water with full force, and the pail was beautifully rinsed out. Then outdoors into the sun to dry. The hot water was supplied by a small coal stove that Tom tended as he went back and forth to the cow barn.

To emphasize the importance of cleanliness in the dairy—and be advised that cleanliness was not the fetish then that it is now—we wore long white aprons and white Dutch caps when working there. Mother made these, no doubt from Dad's design. It was a spotless place.

The Duval separator stood near the sink and it was usually Ed who operated it. The theory was that of centrifugal force which sent the heavier milk particles flying to the outside of the container. We ended up with large buckets of frothy skim milk and smaller buckets of rich yellow cream. All this was done after the whole milk had been bottled. Nobody got skim milk on Dad's farm. This went to the pigs who lived in happy and muddy majesty at the far west end of the Farm.

The cream went into the cooling room—again Dad's invention, as near as he could get to the springhouse of his youth. There was a pool in the cement floor some two feet deep in which water trickled in and out continuously so it was always deep-well cool. The cans of milk and cream stood waist-deep in here. Windows all around kept a circulation of air.

When enough cream had accumulated, either Mother or Lady Newton made butter. The churn was not the nursery rhyme kind but a barrel-type arrangement that swung on a heavy framework. By means of a handle this barrel was swung over and over so the cream was kept in constant motion and eventually the butter particles came together and the sound changed from a sloshing to a thumping and the butter had "come."

Most of the buttermilk was expelled by pressing the butter over and over with wooden paddles and draining off the liquid. Then the butter had to be worked. Mother and Dad evolved a very good system using a big wooden bowl and a big bath sponge covered with cheesecloth. I can still see Mother working the butter—kneading it with her cheesecloth-covered sponge, taking up the moisture, and rinsing and rinsing the sponge. Then she worked in the salt. Mother liked a lightly salted butter. For this reason she did not win prizes at the Riverhead Fair, for Long Islanders salted heavily to make the butter keep longer. Dad said they wanted butter that would keep from clover to clover.

She did, however, win prizes at the Syracuse State Fair, one year the Gold Medal with a nearly perfect score—this against all the butter makers of the upstate dairies. She used no coloring. She didn't need to. Alfalfa-fed cows gave cream that produced butter of a lovely goldfinch color. Her pound pat was displayed in a glass case, well refrigerated. Dad designed the mold and had it made. He was an artist in many ways. As this was to grace the Farm's "Goldfinch Butter," his design was of goldfinches and thistles. Would that I still had it. The *Agronomist* records that Mother's gold medal was won on a rating of $99\frac{1}{2}$ percent but I swear that the $\frac{1}{2}$ turned into $^{99}/_{100}$ over the years for that is the figure I remember. At the National Dairy Show in Chicago she won the Bronze Medal one year, and the Silver Medal another year with a score of 95 percent.

After four years of this kind of winning, she made it at Riverhead and won a first. Not that the butter was any better than ever but the judging standards changed. As Dad said in the *Agronomist*, "long-distance butter" was out.

I was, from this era, hopelessly spoiled by pounds of delicious butter, quarts of rich milk, and cream that was often so rich and thick that it had to be spooned from the bottle. Cream like this on fat red Chesapeake strawberries or meltingly sweet white peaches was food to make the gods weep.

I am sure Dad designed the Homestead, as he designed everything. The living room took up the whole center section of the house. There were identical wide

The Medford farm dairy, covered with climbing roses. ELF wears the white Dutch cap and apron designed by HBF for dairy work.

Dutch doors on the north and south sides. At each side of these doors was a huge window with a deep window ledge. These took up the entire north and south walls. The west side of the room was a huge fireplace made of creamy yellow brick, a heavy mantel, and a chimney breast stepped up to the ceiling to make shelves for knick-knacks.

Under the mantel, on each side of the fireplace, were curio cabinets with glass doors, and these were crammed with mementoes of Dad's past. There were old coins, bits from Mexico, and the old Masonic watch that according to family legend had saved its owner, our seafaring ancestor, from an untimely death at the hands of pirates. One of these cases also contained the emblem of the Whirling Dervishes, that small and exclusive cycling group from the days when Wheelmen were much admired.

The coat rack was another object of Dad's design. It was made of heavy wood, cut out in the form of a graceful F and bedecked with horns. There were deer horns, cow horns, buffalo horns, and a fine spread of steer horns at the top. Coats hung informally by the loops at the back of the neck. Hats perched precariously. It was hard on coats and an object to avoid if you didn't want to be gored, but we found it quite satisfactory.

The horn coat rack designed by HBF

On one of the wide sills of the north windows sat my dolls and stuffed animals—all twenty-one of them—till I was old enough to put them away. In this corner was a hot-air register and the barrel chair, a fine place to sit and warm the feet. The barrel chair was made to Dad's specifications as remembered from his youth. It was indeed a barrel, cut halfway down and halfway across, and upholstered. It was compact and looked nice but it was not noted for comfort.

On the other north windowsill Dad did his printing. All his pictures were done by daylight printing. He was constantly forgetting or being sidetracked which resulted in a lot of overdone photographs.

A woodbox was built in under this window, and beside it, against the stair railing, stood the old Sleepy Hollow chair. It was where Dad sat to read or nap when he wasn't at his desk or steaming around the countryside. It was where I read

"The littlest girl and an All-Head cabbage." Eleanor and a cabbage grown at the Wading River farm, 1906

away the hours too. I could curl up in it in utmost comfort and one book followed another through my youth with many a re-reading of my favorites. In the living room bookcase was a set of Kipling and one of O'Henry, and also one of Stevenson beautifully bound in leather. All of these I read over and over. After I outgrew the Dorothy Dainty books, the Oz books took a lot of time, as did the Rover Boys and Tom Swift. We shared these latter with Harry Newton and when we got hold of a new one it was an occasion for great rejoicing.

Both front and back, the width of the living room, was a deep porch. The one in the back was just a bare slab of cement with full-width steps. I don't think it was planned this way but it became Dad's photographic studio. Here he could line up a few Home Hampers or a choice collection of squash and pumpkins or even a few baskets of strawberries. Since it had a north light it was perfect. He would set up the five-by-seven camera in the middle of the path, fuss for hours on the setup and composition, and then take his pictures. Then off to the darkroom in the cellar to develop and evaluate—and perchance take more.

He liked to have people even in a composition of onions and cauliflower, and would enlist anybody handy. It did result in a fine collection of pictures of us kids, even if only in the role of supporting actor with a cabbage playing the lead. That one of me, aged four, with the enormous head of cabbage in a wheelbarrow was one of his most popular pictures.

The front porch was roofed over and had heavy trellis work designed to carry climbing roses. Across the front was a Gardenia rose, one of my favorites. It was a semi-double soft gold rose that faded to cream but it was a glory when it first opened in the morning. You could reach a few from the ground but the best were on top so I went out the window of Loring's room and down the porch roof when

The front porch of the Medford Homestead *Photograph by EFF*

I needed Gardenias—and I always needed them. They were one of my favorites, with a delicate perfume all their own. A Dorothy Perkins, the well-known little pink cluster rose, grew across the east side and above the dining room window.

All this growth made the front porch a very shady, rather musty spot in summer and every once in a while a little screech owl chose to sit out the daylight hours in this dense shade. We would creep out and peek at him, being careful not to frighten him, and at dusk he would fly off about his owl business.

In the fall the roses shed their leaves and the sun poured in. Then the whole porch was glassed in and it became the garden room. Dad designed sturdy benches with bottoms of heavy, small-meshed wire. They must have been six inches deep and were filled with sphagnum moss. Pots were set into this, Kenilworth ivy and wandering Jew made themselves at home in the moss, and the whole became a green jungle. Asparagus fern drooped plumes or climbed up strings in the corners, a huge abutilon bloomed and bloomed, getting larger each year, and pots of bulbs followed each other from January to spring. We watered with a hose, misted the whole place on a sunny day, and the plants throve mightily. The only heat came from the sun and from the living room through the open door but on really cold nights the little round oil stove was kept lighted out there.

In the fall Dad potted bulbs—all sorts of daffodils, tulips, hyacinths, freesias, and cyclamen. The cyclamen and freesias must have gone straight to the porch but the others were held in his photographic darkroom in the cellar where they rooted and started top growth. By March it was a constant procession of pots coming up with fat buds eager for the sun.

The dining room contained the long table and heavy, black-leather-covered chairs. One china closet was full of the good china and the quantities of cut glass that had been wedding presents and another held ordinary gear. A sideboard held

"Our biggest girl and Japan's biggest radish."
Hope holds a Sakurajima radish, 1907

the heavy silver fruit dishes, silver coffee pots and chocolate pots—also wedding presents. On the wall hung one of Dad's prize-winning photographs of a haying scene, and the portrait of the old "Admiral," as well as the cuckoo clock that Dad wound last thing at night.

The kitchen was Mother's special pride. She had a hand in planning it and she felt it was the last word in comfort and convenience and efficiency for the housewife. It was an improvement on the dark, inconvenient kitchens found in so many farm homes but a modern kitchen efficiency expert would cringe. Nobody had thought of built-ins in 1910 and the wall-to-wall cabinets with drawers for this and slots for that were as much a dream of the future as was an electric stove.

Mother was lucky. She cooked on a coal stove, not wood. The oven was always hot, and a mere shift of the drafts would increase the heat. Much good bread came out of that oven at Medford. A big black Glenwood range it was, and there never was anything cozier than a coal stove with the kettle pluming gently. That was what I missed most when I finally gave up my own coal stove in 1943— the kettle of hot water always to hand. It was a bit of a security blanket, something you could count on. Unless, of course, you forgot to stoke the stove or damp it down. In either case the fire went out. Of course it was dirty, and it was not always easy to persuade someone to get another bucket of coal from the cellar, and somebody had to be dragooned into taking out the ashes once a day. These coal ashes were great stuff when the paths were icy, and they made a good roadbed when they had been pounded into the driveways.

Baked beans should always be done in the oven of a coal stove. You set the pot in after supper and let it simmer all night long. It smelled great when you came downstairs in the morning. Indian pudding and custard baked slowly when the fire was banked. The morning cereal cooked all night in the double boiler—real oatmeal (not rolled oats) or our own wheat cracked at the Yaphank mill and cooked to a nuttiness you wouldn't believe. With the grand thick cream from the dairy this was indeed a meal to start the day right.

Above the stove was the warming oven where the plates warmed up before a meal. On top of the warming oven Mother often had a four-quart pail of milk "setting" for cottage cheese, or bread dough rising in a big brown bowl wrapped in a piece of an old woolen blanket.

Mother also had a fireless cooker, an interesting piece of equipment that she learned about from Cornell by way of the Home Bureau. This organization was a great thing for farm women. It gave them a chance to meet and talk over problems and learn new ways. Mother had a big influence in establishing the Suffolk County Home Bureau and she was its first president. She and Mrs. Archibald Brown of Stony Brook—Helen Parrish Brown of the Southampton Parrishes—worked together on it and they became good friends. Then Mother set to work to establish a local Home Bureau group in Medford. They met in the Grange Hall and the sociability meant as much to the Medford women as all the things they learned, from making slip covers to building and using a fireless cooker.

This cooker was an insulated box with two wells lined with heavy aluminum. You heated two round blocks of soapstone in the oven, inserted one into a well, set in the pan of food, and put the other block on top. You clamped the insulated cover in place, and there your macaroni and cheese or stew or bread cooked away in this trapped heat. The bread was made in three three-cornered pans which fitted into a well. It came out rather steamy and with a soft crust but it was good and we got used to three-cornered slices.

The whole efficient dream kitchen was written up for *Country Life in America* magazine. It seems to have been a stroke of genius to put hooks above the drainboard so various bits of equipment could hang. A shallow shelf under the sink for wrapping paper is mentioned proudly. All the rest of the wide open space under the sink and drain boards just collected dust around the big wooden box that held the burnable rubbish. Garbage went to the chickens as it collected, provided it was to their taste. Otherwise there were the pigs to attend to it. There were few cans and fewer bottles. You could always dig a hole at the edge of the woods and inter what would not burn or could not be eaten.

The real modern feature of Mother's kitchen was the Hoover kitchen cabinet. In this wonder there was cabinet space above with shelves for baking

ELF in the new, modern kitchen at Medford

powder, coffee, cocoa or what you chose, and space below for baking pans, pots and bowls. Inside the door of the lower cabinet was a pot lid rack which was the joy of my eldest when we visited in later years. She would select two lids to carry around in her self-propelled stroller and of course, in order to make a sensible choice, she had to haul them all out, so pot lids would be strewn from hither to yon.

The cabinet had a bread drawer and a drawer for bulky hand tools like the egg beater and the meat grinder. A pull-out, zinc-covered work shelf was in the middle, and in the open space behind this and below the upper cupboards were the flour and sugar bins and the revolving spice rack.

I still use the spice jars from my own Hoover cabinet. For some very odd reason, I can still remember the day I proudly wrote the labels and marked the ginger, clove, cinnamon and allspice jars. I can see myself standing there writing them in the new kitchen in the new house at Middle Island in 1925. Many years ago I made new labels for them as they were getting rather blurry after some forty years of use, but I couldn't bring myself to take off the old labels. They were too much a part of the twenty-three-year-old me who had written them. So I put the new labels on the other side of the jars.

The utility room was next to the kitchen—a largish room with hooks on one wall for coats, a tool board under the window for hanging hammers, screwdrivers

Loring, with Rogue, on the redesigned whalebone seat at
Medford, c.1913

and such, and bins below that for nails, screws, and other small items. Over in one
corner was a wash basin and a toilet. So we had downstairs facilities in a fairly
informal setting.

Upstairs we had four bedrooms, the bathroom, and a very wide hall that took
up the north side. There were three windows with storage chests under them. This
was Mother's sewing room, among other things, and here she would work on
white things when the August days reached that humid heat that laid her low. She
said working on white was cooling. Since she made all our underwear, hemmed all
the table linen by hand, made the kitchen towels and Lord knows what else, there
was always white to work on.

My room was in the northwest corner where the path that was the major
artery of the whole Farm passed the house. I was able to keep in touch with things
from here (including Tom's final trip to the cow barn each night) although my
waking hours were mostly spent outdoors—at least in summer.

The hard-shelled almond tree stood below my window and one of the joys
of spring was watching it come into bloom. From the time the buds began to swell,
through the fat pink-bead stage to the gaudy froth of full bloom, I watched it and
loved it. And always, each year without fail, the first oriole came when the almond
was in bloom. One morning there he would be, sending out his rippling song and
making the most shocking color scheme with his orange and black amidst the pink.

I loved the night sounds. I was not a child who fell into bed and dropped off to sleep. It took time for my mind to run down so I lay and listened to the wind whistling in the screen, or the toads burr-r-ring around the pool, or the owls in the distance, or the whip-poor-wills, often so close you could hear the click before the first "whip." This was whip-poor-will country and, as far as hearing could reach, you could hear their continual calls overlapping each other into the distance. We found one occasionally, getting his daytime sleep under a bayberry bush.

We usually had a night dip in the pool. Dad had built this pool behind the milk house with the idea that he could use it as an ice pond where he could cut ice to store for summer use. But no ice house was ever built. The bottom of the pool sloped from one end to the other, and little corner steps had been built at the shallow end, so I think he meant it to be a swimming pool for us from the beginning but it looked better on the farm plans to call it an ice pond. We enjoyed it thoroughly, actually learned to dog paddle, and slept the better for a cooling dip at bedtime.

We got awfully daring one year. It was the era of the old-style bathing suit with the sailor collar, puffed sleeves, pleated skirt over full bloomers, and

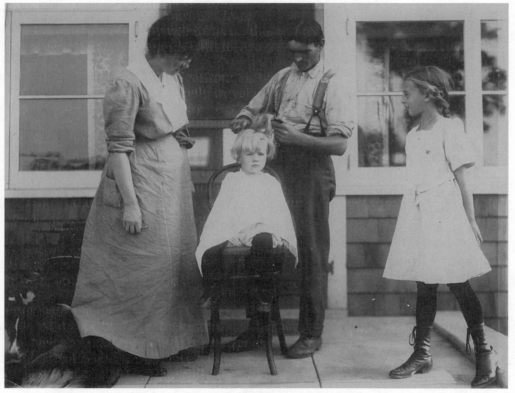

ELF and Eleanor watch Loring's first haircut. One of the Medford farm workers, Teddy Tuddenham, acts as barber. c.1912

stockings. Then along came the glamorous aquatic star, Annette Kellerman, and she introduced a new garment to go under the suit—a sort of body stocking. This was even named the Annette Kellerman. For all I know she performed in this daring garment. We adopted it although I have no idea why we needed something more under our regular suits. Then we conceived the shocking idea of swimming at night—*dark* nights—in the Annette alone. This of course called for raincoats to cover us going and coming from the pool and it also called for much squealing and giggling at our recklessness. It was great—that feeling of freedom in the water. The weight of the regular bathing suit was appalling. It was made of heavy wool and when soaking wet it was not what you could call buoyant.

My favorite after-swim, before-bed snack was a hearty dish of Grape Nuts with cream—spooned out of the bottle. When I was really in a famishing state, a dash of raspberry jam on top gave me the quick energy I needed to get me upstairs to bed. One night we were sitting in Hope's room having a bedtime snack of banana ice cream and in the middle of our feasting the dog ran down a skunk in the immediate vicinity. We put aside our ice cream in a hurry and I have never since been able to even consider eating banana ice cream.

As for the ice, I don't know where we got it. They cut it on the Yaphank lakes, I know, so perhaps someone down there stored it and sold it. One of Dad's favorite expressions was, "That doesn't cut much ice." *We* knew what it meant.

I must have been about eleven when my mother's father, John Alonzo Jones, reappeared in our lives. He had remarried and had a second daughter, Catherine. I remember the day he and Aunt Catherine came out to the Farm at Medford. He was an elegant dresser in his day and I can still remember the white piping on his vest as well as his beautiful curly white hair and curly, full white beard. He was smitten by me, apparently, for he went down on his knees, took me by the shoulders and gazed at me long and soulfully. With tears in his eyes he murmured, "Little Nell." It would seem I was the image of his lost Eleanor Louise.

Dad needed a resident mechanic to keep the pumping and electrical systems going, so Granddaddy moved to Medford. He had a cottage to himself, came over to the Homestead for meals, nursed the pump along, sat in the sun and smoked his pipe for hours at a time, and then retired to his cottage for more hours of meditating—"looking at a mark" was Dad's description. It was I who referred to him as a Badger retreating into his hole and the name stuck ever after.

He was an inventor and held about 30 patents. The one he considered most important was a seal for vodka bottles that he sold to the Russian government. For some years he worked for the Borden dairy company and I remember two of his inventions for them. One was a puncher-server for evaporated or condensed milk cans. A photograph of this, taken by HBF, appeared on his letterhead. The second one was a bottle cap with a flange to cover the lip of the bottle. This was known as the "Kiss Cap—It Covers the Lip." I do believe my Dad came up with that one, and it certainly would be a credit to Madison Avenue.

ELF's father, John Alonzo Jones, better known as Badger. In this 1923 photograph, he holds Eleanor's first child, Edith Eleanor

Medford in those days was a minute village with a railroad station, a post office in the general store, and Hollman's Hotel. We had to be pretty self-sufficient and Mother had to act as doctor, nurse, and social worker. It was she who saved the life of a small girl who got hold of the spoon used to measure out a nicotine spray. Henrietta licked off the spoon and then came around the corner of the pump house, turned blue, and dropped at Mother's feet. Emetics and hot baths brought her around but her own mother could only scream and wring her hands. It was my mother who took charge and had the emergency under control by the time the child's father got back from Patchogue with the doctor. That trip behind a horse must have seemed a long one to him.

I haven't the remotest idea who ever stayed at Hollman's Hotel but the bar did a good business. There was an aged soul named Pop Summers who lived just east of us. He had a shock of unkempt gray hair and a neglected beard. He was bent and bowlegged from years of hard work but every day he walked the two miles to Medford and the Hotel for his mug of beer. Then he walked the two miles back.

As for young people for companionship, there were none. We had little in common with what young folk there were in Medford. If we had gone to school with them it might have been different, but as it was, they lived their lives and we lived ours.

Jeanette spent a lot of time with us in the summers and then there were four of us. Otherwise we were three, and three can be a difficult number. Hope was three years older than I, which seemed more of a gap than the six years between Loring and me. Loring was a joy, and when he got beyond the baby stage he became my playmate. He and I were good pals and did a lot of things together, but neither he nor I got on very well with Hope.

Hope had a great head of thick, dark brown, curling hair, pink cheeks and bright eyes. The hordes of visitors to the Farm were enchanted with her and I sank into my colorlessness unnoticed. I should have suffered, and upon these occasions I did, but on the whole I was happy as a lark.

I acquired a bicycle and after a tremendous struggle learned to ride it. Then I spent my days floating from one end of the Farm to the other, checking on the living things, the growing things (especially the stage of ripeness of any fruit) and the state of Nature in general.

I have no recollection of feeling isolated or lonely. I was perfectly happy with things as they were and found life full and satisfying. I had all outdoors to roam, there was all kinds of excitement on the Farm, there were plenty of books to read, and life suited me fine.

Hope, Eleanor, Loring and baby rabbits, c. 1912

When Teddy Roosevelt Came to Dinner

Ralph Peters was the President of the Long Island Railroad. Theodore Roosevelt was the former President of the United States. On August 11, 1910, they both came to dinner.

Ralph Peters was quite a man. Quite a gentleman. He was, in the first place, a southerner from Georgia and I think he was enough the southern aristocrat to enjoy the pomp and circumstance of being a railroad president. He must have had executive ability and business sense to hold down the job so well but I remember him in his role as Visiting Royalty.

He traveled not by private car but by private train. His visits to the Farm were events. Everyone went to meet the train. The gleaming engine with its two white flags that denoted a Special train would come to a halt at the appointed spot with that glorious whoosh of steam and final clank of wheel that was one of the many beauties of a steam engine. The porter in his white jacket and cap would drop down from the President's car, set the step stool in place and hand down the party—Mr. Peters and whatever guests he honored that day. Often Mrs. Peters came along, and one or more of their daughters. Then the Triumphal Progress proceeded down the long path to the house between climbing roses and flower borders.

But not us kids. Eulis, Mr. Peters' porter, would take us aboard and find some ice cream for us and we would marvel at the luxury of a private car. Loring would admire the engine at close quarters where it lay quietly chuffing and puffing like a quiescent dragon. If there was a train due they would back the Special onto the Farm siding, which was good, for it entailed much throwing of switches and waving of signals and the clinking of train wheels on the switch frogs.

Theodore Roosevelt and Dad had been co-workers in the cause of Good Roads and they were certainly kindred spirits—both go-getters and men who traveled on a full head of steam. Dad's spectacular way of doing things must have appealed to Roosevelt. For some reason, he wanted to come out and see how Dad proposed to accommodate his farm help. He was a forward-looking man and Dad's idea of making the Farm a permanent home for his help, instead of just a seasonal job of work, was something new.

Farm help at Medford must have been a problem from the first. There was no local help available. Those who were farmers were fully occupied on their own small farms. This was still the day of subsistence farming when a man made his living by supplying his own needs. He might cut and sell some wood in the winter, or he might raise chickens and sell eggs. He might do a little carpentry or painting on the side, but basically he was busy at home. With a horse or your feet as your sole means of transportation you didn't range far. So Dad imported his help. I have no idea from where. But each married farm worker was to be given one of the portable houses with running water, electricity, stoves and full coalbins, the produce of the Farm as available, and room for his own gardening or chicken raising if he wished. We eventually had three families of farm workers.

So Teddy Roosevelt—ex-President Roosevelt—was to come out to see the Farm. Even though the Homestead was far from finished, Dad decided that his idol, Colonel Teddy, should eat the first meal served there.

The living room was still a carpenters' shop with a huge workbench down the middle and shavings ankle-deep on the floor, so it must have taken some doing. They finished off and painted the dining room, installed window screens, and hung a double mosquito netting in the wide entrance to keep out the flies. The kitchen had to be finished too, and the stove installed. Then my poor dear Mother had to dig out of packing cases the necessities for cooking and serving a dinner for six or eight. I don't remember who they were but there were at least that many around the table.

The dining room furniture appeared, Dad got pictures on the walls, and I suppose Mother made and hung curtains. Table linen, silver, china and glassware were all located, washed and polished and set in readiness. I was too young to be fully aware of the magnitude of this job but I can look back now and imagine what it was like. This was the kind of thing Dad was always doing and Mother quietly went along with it.

I remember well the excitement of the day. Teddy Roosevelt and Dad thought alike and they really struck sparks. They must have had a wonderful day together. According to the *Sun*:

> One of [T.R.'s] characteristics is his capacity for asking questions. He fired thousands of them...but for perhaps the first time in his life the Colonel encountered a man who talked faster than the speed laws allow. [HBF] absolutely outtalked the Colonel, and they had to reach an agreement about that before Mr. Roosevelt was able to secure the information that he was seeking."

Former President Theodore Roosevelt, LIRR President Ralph Peters and ELF on the front porch of the unfinished Homestead at Medford, 1910

What I remember very plainly—and this is strange for an eight-year-old to have noticed—was Mr. Peters' struggle to be the gracious host and also play second fiddle. He was not used to this. When he came to the Farm he was as much the center of attention as any reigning monarch. Of course everybody played second fiddle to the dynamic Roosevelt but here he was trespassing on Mr. Peters' domain.

This feeling reached its peak at the end of dinner. Hope and I were helping with the serving and we had apparently been at work in the kitchen too. During the pause between dinner and dessert, Hope entered carrying a small cake with T.R. in pink icing on top. Colonel Teddy was overwhelmed with pleasure. He was devoted to children and this was obviously a child's tribute. Poor Mr. Peters actually turned green with envy and frustration, at which opportune moment I appeared with an identical cake with R.P. in pink icing. He was so pleased he nearly wept and I think this cleared away some of his frustration and set the tone for a much better afternoon than it would otherwise have been.

The afternoon's entertainment consisted of a trip to the Wading River farm. The trip from farm to farm was made as we always made it at that time—by car. Very few women drove cars in those days. However, Mother could drive, for Dad insisted that a woman could do anything. And it was Mother who was assigned to drive Teddy Roosevelt to Wading River.

Roosevelt was a little shaken, but off they went, with Mr. Peters in back along with Dad and his camera. The route was through Yaphank, north to Middle

The trip between the two farms, from Medford to Wading River. ELF is at the wheel with Theodore Roosevelt in front and Ralph Peters and HBF (right) in the back. 1910.

Island, east to Ridge and then north on Randall Road. Somewhere along in here Dad had found an old logging road that made a shortcut into the back of the farm. It was nothing but a sandy track and ran through cut-over scrub oak and lowbush blueberry wilderness.

As Mother turned onto this track, the Honorable T. Roosevelt clutched his hat wildly and burst out, "My God, Fullerton, does she know where she is going?" According to the *Brooklyn Eagle*:

> After luncheon, Mrs. Fullerton got out the family farm automobile and took the party across country to the other farm at Wading River. It was fifteen miles distant through a wilderness of scrub oak, with only a thin sandy trail to follow....The storm of a day before had washed away the road at Artist Lake, and suddenly the wheels of the machine on one side slid into the water. Colonel Roosevelt made a flying leap and landed in a clump of bushes. The others scrambled out and then dragged the machine to safety.

The *Sun* reported further:

> Mr. Fullerton discovered that inasmuch as only one of the two cylinders was working, a little pushing from behind might help things. Trust the Colonel in a case like that. He heaved for all he was worth and with the help of the others he had the machine going in a jiffy....Mr. Roosevelt had a bully time laboring under the hot sun.

I daresay Roosevelt remembered that day. Varied as his life was, it must have been unique in his experience.

The *Brooklyn Daily Times* summed it up:

> ...if there was a nook or cranny into which he did not insinuate his interested gaze, it was a mighty small one....When he left this place he knew everything there was to know about it, even to the...family history of the farm hands....The Colonel enjoyed every minute of the day, not even excluding the occasions when he had to get out of the automobile....[He] seemed really to delight in putting his broad shoulder to the wheel and helping the balky auto up the hills.

And in the *Tribune*:

> ...he had to jump from a rapidly moving automobile to escape an involuntary bath in a lake. He walked for a mile along a road ankle deep in sand and fought mosquitoes. Altogether he had a lively day, and when he got back here [to Oyster Bay] tonight he grinned delightedly and said it was "Bully, by George!"

"Queens Road." c. 1898

Good Roads Fullerton—Bicycle to Model T

In his younger days, Dad had been an enthusiastic cyclist. In the late 1800s cycling was a tremendous craze and took many forms—speed racing, endurance tests, touring, day cycle trips, or just wheeling around the park. There were bicycle clubs for everyone, including the ladies and High Society. Status sometimes reared its ugly head, and one's social standing could often be judged by the cycle club to which one belonged.

The Whirling Dervishes were apparently the cream of the crop. They had no clubhouse, no by-laws, no dues, and they refused to have any kind of organization. According to the *Brooklyn Citizen*:

> ...the more Bohemian spirits [argued that] there was no use restricting themselves to rules and regulations when they got along so well without them.

What their initiation rites were, no one knows, for they were a strict secret, but "the ceremonials were in keeping with the novelty that surrounds the strange band of riders."

They did have officers. Their duties could not have been arduous; their titles further emphasized their strangeness. The President was called the Crank and there was High Gear, Front Sprocket and Rear Sprocket. Cyclometer was the Secretary, and this office was held by Hal B. Fullerton with great pride. Tool Bag was the Treasurer, although, as the *Brooklyn Citizen* said:

> ...of what use he can be is a mystery when one considers that the organization has no finances.

There was also Repair Kit, a position held by Doc Merritt, "a well-known surgeon" and also a photographer chum of Dad's.

As for meetings, they had their original ways here, too. The time and place were announced by a notice to each member—for instance, under a certain tree at a certain crossroads at Newburgh-on-Hudson at a certain time and date. Off they went on their bicycles up the Hudson as they pleased, forgathered, and returned to the city in a body.

Membership in this club was not easy to attain, and members were viewed with great respect by the cycling fraternity. My Dad's membership in this club was one of his prides. We had the emblem of the Club—odd, oriental-looking letters superimposed on a bicycle wheel. It was made of some dull metal and I daresay Dad designed it.

The League of American Wheelmen was a national organization and I have Dad's membership card for 1900-01. Somewhere along the line he was a candidate for the presidency of the League but, as far as I can find, he never achieved this post. But he was a member of the State Board of officers and a member of the National Assembly.

Good Roads was a term I heard often in my youth. My Dad was known as "Good Roads Fullerton" in many circles, and he was one of the prime movers in the formation of the Good Roads Association of Brooklyn in 1892. The Mayor of Brooklyn and many other city officers were members of this group, as well as W. H. Baldwin, Jr., the President of the LIRR. Mr. Baldwin went so far as to appoint H. B. Fullerton to take charge of the railroad company's arrangements for the building of better roads in the towns and villages along its lines and for the encouragement of residents in these towns in their efforts to improve highways leading to railroad stations.

It was in the sphere of Good Roads that Dad met Theodore Roosevelt. I don't know just how they collaborated, but I'm sure that they got things done, and they did become friends.

The Good Roads Association was influential in securing the Return Cycle Path from Prospect Park to Coney Island. To celebrate the opening of this path, a mammoth bicycle parade with thousands of riders was held on June 27, 1896. A whole page of the *Brooklyn Eagle* was given to it. The Grand Marshal "sat his wheel like a Major General." His Chief of Staff wore a "crash cycle suit." Then came the banners of the League of American Wheelmen and the Good Roads Association, then the bugler and the orderly and the Grand Marshal's staff of aides and the Parade Committee—among whom rode Hal B. Fullerton.

The Brooklyn Bicycle Club won first prize by unanimous decision of the judges. A hundred and twenty men rode in line dressed in white knickerbockers, blue coats and blue caps. The Kings County Wheelmen were mostly on tandems. The Olympic Wheelmen had a band—"All the players rode single wheels holding on with one hand." The Military Section consisted of men of the 23rd Regiment and the 13th Regiment, and the Good Roads riders numbered "several thousand." One of the novelties of the parade was pictured, a Triple Tandem Sociable—three couples on a seven-wheeled bicycle.

Hope and Eleanor on a country road, c. 1905

To get out of the city and out on the Island for their bicycling jaunts, many cyclists traveled by train. During the summer of 1897 the LIRR carried 150,000 bicycles in its baggage cars and encountered problems both in loading and in unloading. HBF was assigned to solve these problems. He had special railroad cars outfitted with racks to hold the bicycles, with room for the cyclists too. The LIRR ran the first complete bicycle train—six of these cars, each equipped to carry 149 wheels. Racks installed on station platforms further expedited and simplified matters for the wheelmen.

There were general rules for cycling but there was always the show-off who would scorch along at fifteen miles an hour and would weave in and out of traffic, generally showing little courtesy and consideration for the more sedate riders. Finally, a volunteer corps of Cycle Path Police was recruited. Hal B. Fullerton was one of twenty wheelmen selected. The Parks Commissioner wrote to the Good Roads Association on April 15, 1896:

> The twenty wheelmen whom you recommend for special duty on the Cycle Path and in the Park...will have all the powers of the regular police force of the Parks Dept. In other words, they can make arrests....
>
> I sincerely hope that you will take every care to select discreet men, for more harm is often done by overzeal in matters of this kind than is occasioned by permitting an occasional slight offense to go unnoticed....

He was probably right. When a volunteer Park policeman had to resort to running into a scorcher, or spilling him into the gutter to stop him, tempers were bound to run high.

The Brooklyn Cycle Show was held in March of 1897 at the Armory building at Hanson Place and Flatbush Avenue. As the magazine *Brooklyn Life* described it, it was "a most complete exhibit of wheels and equipments." Among these "equipments," wooden handlebars are mentioned and

> ...the hose-pipe tire again is in the lead, but the demand for a double tube tire of detachable outer shoe type is growing....A little instrument for gauging speed is shown and appears to be a good thing.

Mud guards were demonstrated on a wheel spinning in a trough of mud, and a cycle built on new and revolutionary lines was subjected to several severe tests to show its strength to the onlookers. "This responded by breaking in two."

But, alas, no clothing for the cyclist:

> One searches in vain for garments designed for the cyclist—for woolen stockings with cotton feet the same color, for a shoe that will not look like a mitten after a week of wear, a cap properly ventilated, and a suit designed for cycling...a knickerbocker rather than the fulsome bloomer, undergarments with short sleeves or short legs.

A North Shore road, c. 1898

Now these wished-for stockings bring to mind the stockings that Dad always wore. Mother knitted them and I daresay they were invented by the two of them to fill this cyclist's need. Dad always wore knickerbockers so these knit stockings were knee length and they had no foot—just a strap under the instep. Under them he wore cotton socks.

In 1899, the State Legislature passed an act that provided a Sidepath Commission for each county. A 1900 clipping from a Patchogue paper reads:

> The Suffolk County Sidepath Commission has provided for the bicycle rider some of the finest paths to be found anywhere.
>
> Going east along the South Shore [from] Amityville...to Amagansett, there is a continuous path, two or three short gaps excepted. In places these paths are narrow and rough, but...as a rule they form a wide, smooth, level highway for the silent steed. The distance, about 78 miles.
>
> Should the rider wish to return by the North Shore he must needs cross Shelter Island....Once across the north ferry to Greenport he finds the best cycle path in the county—the twenty-three mile stretch into Riverhead.... Between Smithtown and Northport, even though he has a choice of going through Kings Park or Commack, he is either way at the mercy of the county road.

The roads were often referred to as "soft." As I remember it, they were either soft with sand or with mud, and they could be abominably rutted and abominably dusty. Road conditions over a wide geographic area were published in the newspapers as snow conditions are now for ski enthusiasts.

Several cross-island cycle paths were built. Among them was the fourteen-mile path from Port Jefferson to Patchogue, which I knew well in my youth. It was a raised path, certainly only wide enough for two bicycles, and it ran just west of the Experimental Farm at Medford into Hagerman. We rode it happily on our bikes but without competition. By our day, people were doing their scorching in automobiles and the bicycle no longer was the last word in speed and sport.

Bicycle tags were required. These cost $1.00. In 1899 and 1900, $18,000 was collected, all of which was used to maintain the paths. In 1901, tag number 3 was issued to HBF "in recognition of the work done by him for the Commission."

In 1901 a Pan American Exposition was held in Buffalo and the management set out to lure the country's cyclists. Routes were carefully detailed for those cycling from Boston, New York, Philadelphia, Washington, Baltimore, Pittsburgh, Cincinnati, and even Milwaukee. The route from Schenectady to Buffalo that was most highly recommended was the route also chosen for the Endurance Test of the Automobile Club of America scheduled for September of the same year. The guideposts for this automobile run were erected under the supervision of HBF and no doubt he put them up in time to be of assistance to the cyclists too.

Not a man to miss an opportunity, my Dad also took advantage of the occasion to rally the Good Roads brethren with the idea of organizing a statewide Good Roads Association. The *Buffalo Commercial* says:

> He will undoubtedly succeed for he is one of those men who seldom fail in anything.

We heard the story of Mile-a-Minute Murphy's ride over and over during my childhood and it made the ride of Paul Revere a tame episode by comparison. On June 30, 1899, Charles Murphy made cycling history by riding a measured mile in 57.8 seconds—and he did it behind a LIRR train.

Murphy was a policeman and a champion cycle rider. He held many speed records and evolved a theory that there was no limit to the speed a man could make on a bicycle, provided "wind pressure" could be eliminated. He declared he could keep up with a railroad train at any speed it could achieve if he had a smooth track behind the train and a hood to protect the bicycle. His theory was that "the fast moving locomotive would expel the air to such an extent that I could follow in the vacuum behind." He added, "Remember that a vacuum is not suction, it is the absence of air."

For thirteen years he made this challenge and tried to get the cooperation of some railroad. At last he met the right man—Hal B. Fullerton. Anything that would focus attention on cycling appealed to Dad. Then Murphy suggested that if the LIRR would set up this race, they would win fame too. They would "...prove to the world that they had just as good rolling stock, roadbeds, and employees as any other railroad in the world."

This was indeed a sore spot. As one newspaper put it:

> The LIRR in 1899 was the butt of jokes in witty columns, on vaudeville stages and in joke books. Audiences and readers got the distinct impression that a young man embarking on the LIRR at Patchogue for New York was a decrepit graybeard before he reached Jamaica.

HBF was the railroad publicity man and he was indeed a publicity man par excellence. Here was a stunt that would capture the public's enthusiastic attention, which could be equally divided between Murphy and the mighty LIRR.

A section of track was chosen at Maywood, near Babylon, and boards were laid between the rails for three miles. The Engineer and the Fireman were chosen, and Murphy graciously stated in his account of the affair that Sam Booth, the Engineer, and Fireman Howell "have won glory among railroad men as being in the champion class." A light locomotive was first used but it could not achieve Murphy's desired speed of a mile a minute. They finally brought in the heaviest and fastest locomotive the railroad owned, and the gallant Booth and Howell were able to fire her up to the required mile in sixty seconds.

The engine pulled one car and this was filled with all the railroad Big Brass as well as the representatives of the press and the officials involved in the race— timers, announcer (with megaphone), attending physician, and the general manager of the whole affair, Hal B. Fullerton. There were many who were very dubious

Where the Cross-County Cycle Path crossed the tracks at Medford, 1897. The sign warns, "Steam Railroad Crossing." *Courtesy of Suffolk County Historical Society*

Mile-a-Minute Murphy begins his historic ride behind a LIRR train, 1899. *Courtesy of Suffolk County Historical Society*

of the whole thing, considering it utterly foolhardy, impossible, and more than a little dangerous. Dad used to tell how the President of the railroad—Mr. Potter, I believe it was—refused to watch, and sat inside the car in much trepidation.

The route was lined with spectators. HBF saw to it that the cycling world was well alerted. The event coincided with the mid-summer meet of the New York Division of the League of American Wheelmen, which was being held in Patchogue. This, I am sure, was no coincidence. HBF picked the day with care, and the time was four p.m., giving plenty of time for cyclists to converge from all directions on Maywood. A letter from HBF addressed to the "Cycling Editor" is apparently a form letter sent to all newspapers. It gives detailed instructions on the routes to the site and ends with assurances that he will "make arrangements so that you can get to the wires at the earliest possible moment after the run is over." Dad knew his newspapermen.

Murphy's own description of the race reads like an old-fashioned thriller. He speaks of "riding on dead air—absolutely still atmosphere," but he also says:

> I was riding in a maelstrom of whirling dust, hot cinders, paper and other particles of matter—sucked in under the train apparently.

Here I raise an eyebrow. You can't have it both ways. Of the first quarter-mile he says:

> I was riding against hope. I expected the worst....For the first time I realized that the eyes and minds of people thought my ride was impossible, but the sight of agonized faces on the rear platform yelling, holding out their hands, sent a thrill of determination through me.

He gathered his forces and forged ahead and he could see "a new look of confidence in the faces above me." On he pedaled,

> ...through the fire of hot cinders and rubber [from a rubber shoe at the bottom of the shield rubbing on the rails]. The car was crowded with men who had been used to seeing any and all things that were dangerous, but the howling and screaming of sturdy officials and newspaper men from all over the U.S. that stood on the platform put all on edge.

Near the end of the run he was moving faster than the train itself and he

> ...expected anything. My eyes were glued upon Hal Fullerton, my friend who had made my dream possible to revolutionize railroading and cycling.

As the mile was passed, Sam Booth in the engine shut off the steam and the engine slowed rapidly. Murphy was still pedaling furiously and he crashed into the protecting bar at the end of the train. The two men who crouched there—one of them HBF—reached out to pull him aboard. As Dad told the tale, Murphy said to him quietly, "I'd like to save the bike," wrapped his legs around it and was pulled in, bike and all.

Victory! And, in Murphy's words:

> The excitement among officials and representatives of the press was a sight that will perhaps never again be witnessed. Every man in the car felt that a very remarkable performance had occurred and the general nervous reaction had ended in pandemonium. Grown men hugged and kissed each other. One man fainted and another went into hysterics.

I don't think his achievement "revolutionized railroading" or did much to change cycling, but it made a hero of Murphy and he became known all over the world as Mile-a-Minute Murphy. He lived on this fame the rest of his life. He came to my Dad's funeral and I guess that was the only time I ever saw him, but his story was very much a part of my early days.

Dad was all for progress, and the automobile was progress. In 1901 he had his finger in a hundred-mile endurance test that was laid out by the Long Island Automobile Association. Ten of fifteen cars completed the grueling run from Jamaica to Manhasset and Oyster Bay, south to Massapequa and Freeport, and so back to Jamaica. This was a test of endurance; speed was frowned on and a safe fifteen miles per hour was the order of the day. One car failed in the hill climbing test at Roslyn because the car gave out and the driver had to push it up the hill. Since this driver had been too speedy on this stretch anyway, he was doubly disqualified.

Dr. Herman Baruch was one of the contestants. Albert Bostwick, later of polo fame, did not run because his favorite car (one of seven) was out of commission. On hand at the start, according to an old newspaper clipping, was "Automobile Bill, the repairman, who is to the auto what Bicycle Oliver was to the Wheelmen a few years ago." Fournier, the French racing driver, gave up and went back to the city when a drizzle turned to real rain.

Fournier apparently spent quite a bit of time over here trying for speed records. William K. Vanderbilt was instrumental in getting him, I think. Vanderbilt was a great enthusiast and was responsible for the Vanderbilt Cup Races, as well as the Vanderbilt Parkway where they were run. This private toll road was built for the rich man's sport of automobiling, from the west end of the Island out to Lake Ronkonkoma where there were facilities for wining and dining and reliving the thrills. You can still find a long section of this Parkway running from Dix Hills to Hauppauge.

Fournier was also the driver in the first train versus automobile accident in America. Unfortunately, my father was in the front seat.

"Dosoris Lane at Glen Cove"

This was on October 30, 1901 at the Westbury crossing. When the impact was obviously unavoidable, Fournier and the three other passengers jumped but Dad was wedged in the front seat between levers and his camera gear. The car was thrown clear of the track but Dad suffered a huge scalping wound, and a great splinter from the car's wooden body had to be cut out of his leg. Fortunately the Mineola Hospital was nearby and he had prompt attention and recovered completely. I was born three months later so it must have been a tough time for Mother.

When he got back on his feet, Dad wrote to Mr. Baldwin, who was the President of the LIRR at that time, giving his version of the whole thing. True to his oath of loyalty to the LIRR, Dad's aim was to exonerate the Engineer, the engine, the whole LIRR. In his eyes the whole blame lay on Fournier's shoulders and on the French automotive industry which would let a car take to the road without sufficient braking power to stop such a behemoth going at twelve to fifteen miles an hour. Moreover, he practically apologized for having been so nearly killed and having drawn adverse attention to the railroad. I daresay it was after this that the signs were put up—those open diamonds that warned, "Railroad crossing. Look out for the cars."

Railroad crossings were always taken very seriously when I was young. Unless there was perfect visibility, somebody got out and walked ahead, checked the safety of the moment, and waved the driver on. There was a dandy on the road from Yaphank village to Camp Upton—a hilly, curving road with a crossing where the tracks came through a cut. Visibility was nil for both car and train.

When the Bartlett ladies used to travel with us—this takes us clear up to the thirties and life at Middle Island—conversation would cease as we approached a crossing.

"Maud!" Agnes would speak firmly, "Don't distract Eleanor's attention!"

And Maud would manage to cease her delightful prattle while we negotiated the perilous single-track, level crossing at the Yaphank railroad station.

Anything "going by" in my youth was an occasion. Everyone checked each horse-drawn rig as it passed to see who it was and guess where they were going. When automobiles began to sputter and wheeze along the roads they were definitely checked through. Small boys might cheekily shout, "Get a horse!" but they would hope that it might be their horse that would be needed so that they could get a closer look. Oldsters might frown at such unwonted speed, and solemn-faced solons might pass laws against "scorching," but the cars were worth looking at.

Since Dad believed the automobile was here to stay, and since he had distances to travel, the railroad bought a car for the Farm. This first one was bought while we were still in Huntington. I went along to Hicksville to get it. It was a Brush and a mere skeleton of a car. It turned out to be highly temperamental. I have vague recollections of a great struggle even getting it home that day, and I have less vague

HBF driving the IHC, the International Harvester farm wagon, 1913

recollections of the many times it broke down thereafter—on the hill between the Farm and Yaphank, in the wilderness north of the Wading River farm, and clear out in Mattituck one day.

Then there was the time when we were all bowling along through Smithtown on the way to a day with the dentist in Huntington and the inevitable happened. Mother, Hope and I spent the day with the Pardingtons while Dad and his pal of cycling days, Charlie Pardington, ran around getting the car repaired. This problem child was called the Mud Turtle.

When the International Harvester Company came out with a real farm wagon, the Mud Turtle went, and we acquired the IHC which did duty for many years. It was a high-wheeled, hard-tired, two-cylinder, air-cooled job with front and back seats, and not even a windshield to cut the wind. True, the wind of our going was not overwhelming as twelve to fifteen miles per hour was our cruising speed. When Dad was in a real hurry or feeling downright devilish he would speed up to twenty, at which Mother would clutch her side of the seat and say firmly, "Hal!" At that, Dad would drop back to a safe fifteen. This creation was called the Locust.

It was a thing of beauty and a joy—sometimes. It was far from 100 percent reliable. Its usual trick was to break a fan belt, and Dad became good at this particular repair. Actually he had very little mechanical know-how but he adored problems and was not averse to making quite a production of solving them. I am sure Mother groaned inwardly and suffered with these long waits, and we kids got desperately tired, but there were always blueberries or trailing blackberries or wintergreen berries to ferret out and eat, sassafras bark and leaves to chew, and even a box turtle now and then to keep things lively. To us it was just the way it was.

The IHC wasn't bad for summer travel or for good weather but a cold day in January with a booming north wind coming across the flats on the back road that went from East Patchogue through Hagerman, and then straight north to the Farm, left much to be desired. I don't know how Dad and Mother stood it up front without a windshield to break the blast. The rest of us went to earth in back under the buffalo robe. We had two of these buffalo robes—yes, real American bison—so I guess Mother retreated behind the other. Dad found an old foot warmer that Mother sometimes used. Whoever made that little square box with the pierced tin sides never dreamed that the hot coals would some day warm the feet of a lady riding in a gasoline buggy.

The IHC had kerosene head and tail lights and it was a good idea to keep them in mind and be sure they were full. Come dusk you just stopped, struck a match and lighted up—if the lamps had been refilled after the last night march.

You may have laughed heartily over the poor man who was disqualified in the Endurance Run because he had to push his car up the hill at Roslyn, but this was quite standard procedure. There were plenty of hills we never *expected* the car to make to the top unaided. The one east of Middle Island just west of Lustgarten's Nursery was a case in point. This was known as the Camel's Hump and Dad just

The IHC with Pennsy providing added horsepower

slowed down a trifle at the foot so we could all pile out. This lightened the car so she would make it part way up and when she faltered we all put the shoulder to the wheel and pushed the rest of the way. On rare occasions Dad would give it a try—race up to the hill and give her all she had. Once or twice he made it and the hurrahs rang through the underbrush. East Broadway in Port Jefferson was the hill-climbing test for cars for years. It is still a long pull but hardly a challenge.

On the trip from Medford to Wading River the half-way stop was Pfeiffer's Store in Middle Island. There we "filled her up." Mr. Pfeiffer would produce a five-gallon can of gas, a large funnel, and a large square of chamois. The gas tank was under the front seat so it all had to be hoisted up. While the gas gurgled through the chamois into the tank we would go into the store and Mrs. Pfeiffer would sell us some big fat cookies out of a cookie keg. Jumbles were the favorite—ginger cookies, soft and with sugar on top. We got root beer too so this was a very fine road stop for us kids. Mr. Pfeiffer also had an IHC and we compared notes.

Finally, Henry built his Ford and the Model T came to the Farm. The luxury of this car was overwhelming. A roof, a windshield, and side curtains that could be let down "in case of a change in the weather." It still had to be cranked and it had to be pushed up the Camel's Hump but I believe the cruising speed rose to 25 miles per hour which really expedited things. There seemed to be a lack of quality control at the Ford factory for we had good ones that gave little trouble and we had a couple that were always problems.

Starting a Ford could be a real hassle. The deft twist of the crank and the instant response was a pipe dream. You cranked and cranked; you advanced the spark and you retarded the spark; and then you got someone young and strong— Ed Newton was first choice—to "spin the crank." This was around and around as fast as you could do it and sometimes it worked. Of course it was known, on occasion, to backfire and break an arm.

When it was deemed hopeless, all hands started pushing. Many is the time I have taken my place at a rear fender and helped push a Model T from the back door up to the main road.

But there were times when it would run like a breeze and we would sail along in great style. We kids liked to ride on the front mudguards—fenders to you—one on each side, on our stomachs, clinging to a headlight. We really saw where we were going.

Of course Mother drove this superior vehicle, and Hope and I both learned to drive. I got my license in 1920. It does rather give people pause when I remark that I learned to drive in a Model T.

The road between Medford and the Farm, which Dad called Prosperity Boulevard, was a one-lane track that was a challenge on every trip. In spots it was clayey so it was muddy in winter and spring but mostly it was plain sand—sand ruts with the sand up to the axles of the IHC or the farm wagon. There were places where a fellow could turn out if an intrepid voyager appeared going in the opposite

HBF, Loring and ELF on Prosperity Boulevard, c.1911

direction but it was not always easy. There were two hills to contend with. Neither would be noticeable nowadays and the one nearest the Farm, Pine Dell, was fairly easy. The other one, just west of Humpety-Slumpety-Slew-Telegraph Curve, could require manpower—or kid power—on occasion. Humpety-Slumpety was a spot where the road wound itself around a telegraph pole for some unknown reason and was very greasy when wet. It was a great day when this curve was straightened out.

In the summer of 1912 Prosperity Boulevard was put into such condition that it could finally be called a road. However, it was not all sweetness and light. It was fine for us to get around with speed and ease—usually—but so did other people, and more and more of them found their way to the Farm by road. This should have meant that they could *go* by road instead of having to wait for the four o'clock train but it didn't really work out that way. Once anyone was there, Dad made of them a captive audience and Mother would sigh quietly and set a couple of extra plates for lunch.

What we really disliked were the busloads of "summer people" from Patchogue. This was the era of the summer hotel and there were two in Patchogue, the Clifton House and the Ocean Avenue Hotel. Both were big sprawling affairs right on the Bay. It was the custom for Mama and the kiddies to spend the summer at one of these glorified boarding houses and Papa would take the LIRR on Friday night and join them for the weekend. Then they would take the ferry across to Cherry Grove, have a huge shore dinner at the Cherry Grove Hotel, and disport themselves on the beach for the day.

During the week the mamas and kiddies, the elderly and the maiden ladies were not overwhelmed with amusements. Their sewing and gossiping and rocking on the veranda might be varied by a bus trip up to Main Street and they might make a small purchase at the drugstore or the five-and-ten, or they might go to a movie.

Occasionally a bus trip was organized and they went on an exciting expedition to see the LIRR Experimental Farm at Medford. These buses couldn't have carried more than eighteen or twenty people. They were mostly used to meet the trains and gather in the clients. A long seat ran the length of the bus on each side so it was a vis-à-vis arrangement.

I think most people just went for the ride but when they saw peaches and plums hanging ripe on the trees, raspberries thick on the bushes, or grapes turning blue in great clusters their mouths watered and their fingers itched.

Cries of anguish would go up when we saw a bus arriving, and we scattered in all directions to guard that which was most precious to each. I must have been torn, for everything was choice to me, but I am sure I patrolled the Satsuma plum trees if they were ripening.

We had a housekeeper at one time named Miss Metcalf to whom a Champion peach was the reward for a good life so she made a bee line for the Champion trees when the summer people appeared. Miss Metcalf was a nice person and definitely a lady. She came from Baltimore and I don't know why she came to do housework for us. She was actually an assistant and Mother did as much of the work as she did, but Lord knows Mother needed help around that house with all the outside activities Dad expected of her.

Grading the road at Medford, c. 1911

When Dad and Mother went on speaking trips or to railroad conventions I am sure they felt very content to leave us in Miss Metcalf's care. Another of my strange, clear-cut, fragmentary memories is of having lunch on such an occasion in the garden room on a winter day. We had piccalilli sandwiches and cocoa with whipped cream. We kids must have asked for this, for no adult would dream it up. Ah, for a young digestion.

Miss Metcalf was, I suppose, middle-aged and was tremendously heavy. She also had a tendency to drop off to sleep the minute she sat down. She was a nice addition to the household and she was a dandy cook. Her chicken always had cream gravy, the strawberry shortcake was thick and rich, and the egg beaters whirred often, to my delight, and whipped cream appeared wherever it possibly could. (And if there was any left over I was not above putting it on my oatmeal in the morning.)

As I say, the Champion peaches were her ultimate joy and she protected them like a dragon. Dad was mostly worried when we were approaching fair time for all the choicest specimens of everything were reserved for the fairs.

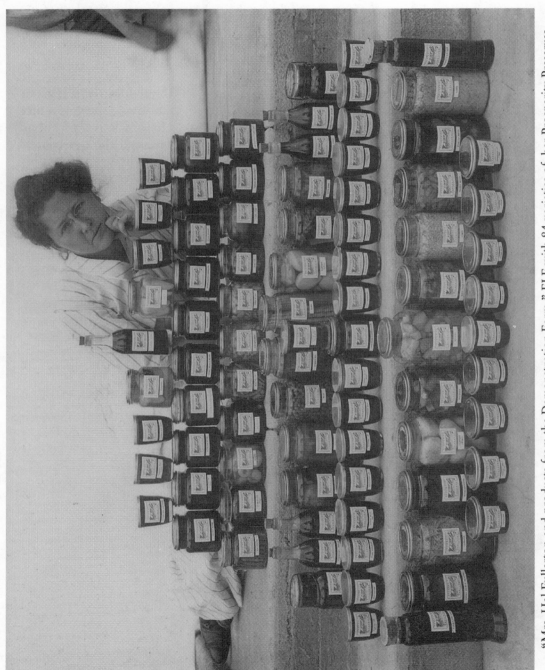

"Mrs. Hal Fullerton and products from the Demonstration Farm." ELF with 84 varieties of her Prosperity Preserves

Fair Week—One After Another

Now that was indeed a month—September, the month of fairs. How Mother survived I do not know, but Dad throve. This was the time when he showed the world what he had achieved on his Blessed Isle. But don't assume that he took his produce to the Suffolk County Fair at Riverhead and called it a day. Oh no. It went like this.

We had a portable house for the fairs. This was transported in a railroad car, and a baggage car was assigned for the produce. When these were first rolled onto the siding we kids dashed up with our bikes, hoisted them in, and rode merrily from one end of a car to the other. We would climb all over the tops of the cars and play train. This was Loring's joy. We could pretend-spin the brake wheel at the end of each car, wave signals back and forth, and make fine engine noises. We traveled far and wide in our imaginations. Then the farm wagon rolled and vast amounts of produce were tenderly packed into the car, along with material for staging. As I have said, Dad was dramatic and any display of his was really staged.

The little house was settled down in the middle of the Riverhead Fairgrounds, with a fenced-in yard, a flower-bordered path, and a token foundation planting, and the two rooms were jammed with Dad's choicest. He always had a setup of pictures to show the ways and means. These were ten-by-twelve-inch transparencies set in wooden frames and lighted from the back. This was long before the day of color photography so Mother hand-colored every one—meticulously, of course, as she did everything. She also colored his lantern slides and this was an even more exacting job.

Of course he had the tallest corn and the biggest pumpkins outside to catch the eye, and people swarmed in the front door and out the back door all day long with Dad declaiming—also all day long—to whomever would listen. And many did.

Part of the exhibit in the Farm's cottage at the county fair

In the *Agronomist* I find Dad's own introduction to fair week, written in his inimitable style:

> It does one good to meet the Long Island neighbors and exchange the hearty handshake, now a lost art except among those who live in the open and act from the heart's impulse, rather than upon the dictation of some self-elected director of social usages.
>
> It jumps one out of the ruts...to see results the other fellow has accomplished and in the swap of the year's experiences learn how all was achieved.

A real old county fair was a tremendous event. Every farmer in the county got to the fair if he could, and usually the whole family went along. They came to gloat over their own winnings or to see what the other fellow had won, or just to see all the biggest and best.

Dad and Mother stayed in Riverhead for the whole week in the early days. Later, when the speedy Model T made it practical, they went back and forth every day, leaving home at the crack of a foggy dawn and getting home after dark.

When they stayed out there they checked in at the Griffin House. At the end of each day they must have eaten supper and fallen into bed. At least Mother did,

I am sure. I know Dad was still going strong, for sometimes we kids spent the week out there too and Dad would take us to the movies in the evening. This I can remember well. It was not a neon-signed movie palace in those days. One walked down a plank sidewalk to some kind of remodeled back building where they had erected screen, projector, and benches for the avid audience. Here we saw Charlie Chaplin and various episodes of a continuing thriller called *The Broken Coin. The Perils of Pauline* had started a rash of these thrillers and it seemed that we were always running into *The Broken Coin.* I haven't the faintest idea what it was all about. I daresay it had a European background and a Graustarkian flavor. Dad always called it "The Busted Coin" and was as thrilled as we were.

He had a delightful, childlike appreciation of such things and his enjoyment was whole-hearted. Charlie Chaplin was a delight to him and he would howl with mirth. When Dad laughed like that the tears streamed down his face and he had such a struggle to keep his eyes open far enough to see what was going on that he amused us as much as Charlie Chaplin did.

He laughed like this when he read something funny too. Reading aloud went on way beyond our early childhood and a good book was often a read-aloud one. Especially a funny one. *Helen's Babies* sent Dad into such paroxysms of mirth that he could hardly get the words out, but at that point we could always pick up the

LIRR President Ralph Peters (wearing gloves) outside the Farm's exhibit cottage at the county fair

book ourselves the next day and fill in the gaps. It's been a long time since I've seen anyone enjoy such wholehearted laughter.

We kids had a fine time at the fair too. We were free to wander far and wide and covered the same paths many times. The vegetables were in one long building, the fruits in another, and flowers in a third. There were wide doors at each end and great long tables down the middle and the sides. Each hall had its own flavor. Vegetable Hall smelled of potatoes and cabbage and onions, Fruit Hall like Persian gardens and exotic Spain, with the perfume of peaches giving place to the aroma of grapes and the delicate odor of Bartlett and Seckel pears. This was a good hall to stroll through. The fruit was protected under chicken wire screens or there might have been gaps in the perfect plates.

Of course Flower Hall should have been my favorite, but it was too heavy with the odor of tuberoses for me. The exhibits consisted mostly of collections from private home gardens although there must have been commercial exhibits too. Long Island had become a great center for florists. The light soil and the proximity to the New York markets made a good combination. The demand for violets was great. They were sold on the streets as well as in the flower shops of New York. More than once Dad bought us violets when we were in the city. He was very prone to buy flowers. Once when Mother, Hope and I were waiting for Dad in the waiting room of the newly erected Pennsylvania Station, he appeared with flowers for each of us. There were roses and violets and sweet peas but I don't remember who got which.

The Women's Building was jammed to the rafters with quilts, bedspreads, tablecloths, children's and ladies' dresses, skirts and blouses. All the good things that can come from a farm or village kitchen—bread, cake, cookies. Jams, jellies, pickles. Canned fruit and vegetables. Butter and cottage cheese.

Mother always entered a large collection of her beautifully packed fruits and vegetables, her jams and jellies, and her butter. All this besides what was on display in the LIRR cottage. How did she do it all?

There were concessions in this building too. You could buy a ring and a man would engrave your monogram right there and then, or another would burn your name in flowing script on a leather wallet or a pocketbook with fringe. We would watch these fascinating men for hours.

Out in the open there were men who sold souvenirs of the fair and balloons and whips. Why should whips be such an attraction? I suppose anyone who drove a horse managed the whip with great éclat and the whip became a bit of a status symbol to a kid. I liked the whips. Each handle was a different color and the lash at the end was rather fun to flick around. I guess it was mostly something to carry around like the malacca cane that Mr. Peters always carried.

The animal section was another part of the fairgrounds and we made regular visits to the animals we liked. I always managed to find a cow or a duck or a Belgian hare that delighted me particularly. I fancied the Bantam chickens. One year I fell madly in love with a Jersey cow and spent hours in her company. I daresay it was

"No. 2's 'Pine Barrens' productions ready for shipment to the Suffolk County Fair." 1910

an unrequited love but Jerseys are very sweet and gentle people and she didn't rebuff me.

The horse racing left me very cold although it attracted hundreds of racing fans. I would hang on the rails and watch the little sulkies careen past but I couldn't understand the hysteria over who won and who didn't. I just didn't relate to horse racing.

We had a hearty noon meal at an interesting restaurant building near the cottage. This looked like the usual dining hall at a summer camp. It was shut up tight for the rest of the year but for fair week the sides opened up and out to form awnings over the wide-open sides. They should have been screened but I'm sure they weren't. The swarms of flies were just taken for granted in those days and a few fly ribbons were hung around as token battle signs. The food may have been protected by fly netting and the butter was in a covered dish but I think otherwise it was every fly for himself. Long wooden tables and long wooden benches made perfectly satisfactory accommodations and the food was hearty and plentiful. At the Griffin House at night we also sat at long tables and the food was passed back and forth family style.

The amusements eluded me as amusements. The merry-go-round I liked in moderation but I would have no part of the rides. I was far from a daring child. The shooting galleries and side-shows of freaks were not for children and it was all very noisy. I preferred to go back and commune with my favorite rabbit.

This went on for six days. And on the seventh day they packed everything back into the baggage cars and moved it all to Mineola. The Nassau County Fair was not as bucolic as the one at Riverhead but Nassau County was very much of an agricultural county in those days. There were acres and acres of market gardens on the rich black soil of the Hempstead Plains. There were also acres and acres of sand violets (*Viola pedata*) that were a haze of lavender in May. All the area east of Garden City that became, in turn, Mitchel and Roosevelt Fields, the huge shopping center and the miles of industrial buildings, was once a glory of sand violets in the spring. It was a joy to travel through on the train. Dad took a picture of Hope marooned in this beautiful sea.

The Mineola Fair had its full quota of agricultural entries including some fine dairy cattle from the estates and good fruit from the North Shore orchards. But the biggest crowds came for the horse racing, and later for the automobile racing. My memories of the Mineola Fair are vague, I think because we never stayed there. We may have put in a day or so but that was all. Dad and Mother stayed at the Mineola Hotel, but not the small fry.

Then, as if that were not enough, they were off to the State Fair in Syracuse. They must have had time to get back to the Farm and regroup for this one. They did not have a cottage at Syracuse, just space in one of the halls. But the staging had to be worked out, the new exhibits chosen, and entries from other Long Island farmers collected. All this went in a special railroad car assigned to carry the Long

Hope in a sea of violets, Hempstead Plains, c.1904

Island exhibits to Syracuse. Dad tells in the *Agronomist* how this car was detached from the LIRR train, shunted onto a barge, and towed by tug around the lower end of Manhattan and up to the New York Central terminal.

The State Fair was always a most impressive thing, for New York is a great agricultural state. Fruit is one of the biggest crops so the fruit exhibits were a sight to see. There were acres of tables full of apples—five to a plate, and each the choicest of the whole orchard. Each prize that came to a Long Island orchardist was grist for Dad's publicity mill: "Long Island orchardist beats the best of the Upstaters!" "No fruit can beat that grown on Long Island!"

Huge bunches of grapes perfumed the air with that fruity essence of autumn. Some of the grape exhibits were astonishing. They made paintings using bunches of grapes as they use roses in the California Rose Parade. One picture of Biblical origin stays in my mind. Dad, with his Bible-reading background, knew the story. It seems Moses sent men into Canaan "to spy out the land" and told them to see if it was rich or poor. He told them to

> ...bring of the fruit of the land. Now the season was that of the first ripe grapes. So they went up and...came unto the brook of Eshcol, and cut down from thence a branch with one cluster of grapes, and they bare it between two upon a staff.

Well, there were the two men, more than life-size and all made of grapes of various colors, with a pole between them, and suspended from it the great-grandfather of all bunches of grapes. I wouldn't know how many bunches it took to make up this huge bunch. It was most impressive.

Dad says in the *Agronomist* that this amazing art work "...was cleverly executed...somewhere in the neighborhood of a ton of these palate ticklers being used in the construction of both the picture and its frame." He also mentions other pictures made of onions or peppers. I do vaguely remember something done with millions of onions.

There were other fairs. There was the Land Congress at Madison Square Garden—the original Madison Square Garden located, strangely enough, at Madison Square. This was in November, 1911. In the *Agronomist* Dad describes it at great length, starting with the following typical blast:

> A glorious gathering together of the North American continent's unri-
> valled natural wealth was for the first time congregated under one roof, and
> that roof in the home town of the greatest number of people in one community
> living upon or off of each other in the world (bar London).

There was the Land Show at the 71st Regiment Armory at 34th Street and Park Avenue in 1912. This was a tremendous affair. Agricultural exhibits from all over the country were set up in elegant style. Dad outdid himself with his display of colored transparencies. It was in late November, so the produce was limited to winter keepers. There were great commercial exhibits and the plow manufacturers vied with the makers of the Planet Junior—that neat little one-man tool that was useful both in home gardens and in the professional market garden. The dairymen were on hand too, and there was one amazing exhibit of a life-sized cow made of butter. She stood in a glass case, well-iced I trust, and was most impressive.

When in New York we stayed at the Hotel Seville on 27th Street. This was a nice family hotel and very Victorian with thick rugs, much red plush, and deep armchairs in the lobby. It was much frequented by Latin American families so the name was well chosen, and Spanish rippled freely through the dining room and the elevators.

I think after the yearly round of fairs Mother was allowed a rest period. I know we went once to Montauk in the fall when the gerardia was rosy all over the downs and this may have been a post-fair vacation.

The Wide-Open Spaces at Montauk

Montauk was the end of the line. The railroad ended at a little station and there was a Y where they turned the engine for the return run. The fishing village was a cluster of houses near the station and the Conklin House stood high on a nearby hill. Beyond that to the east it was wide, rolling downs all the way to the Lighthouse at the tip of the Island.

This great open area was used as range land, and in my youth they brought herds of beef cattle from the west, pastured them here for the summer and, in the fall, took them to the New York market. The downs swept into sand dunes along the ocean front and beach grass took over from the range grass. Beach plum bushes grew in the hollows. What a gorgeous beach it was, miles and miles of clean and untouched sand.

The downs were mostly covered with rough grasses and wildflowers but there were boggy patches where *Azalea viscosa* grew to perfume the air in June. In summer, highbush blueberry carried loads of smoky blue fruit. There were little patches of wind-bonsai'd trees where there was a bit of shelter, and below the Conklin House and near the railroad tracks there was a grand marsh where the red-winged blackbirds nested and called among the cattails. It was there we found the dainty little orchids—ladies' tresses, calopogon, and rose pogonia. A fresh-water pond lay to the south of this swamp and once we were there in early summer when it was completely framed in the blue of wild iris (blue flag). I loved these, for you could find all degrees of blueness in the individual plants and the design at the base of each petal was as exotic and intricate as the decoration on a Persian brass vase we had at home.

It took so little to fill a vacationer's day happily in the early 1900s. There were books to read and embroidery to work on. A little conversation, a gentle walk in the afternoon, the full glory of the sunset over Gardiner's Bay for evening diversion, and bed by nine made a delightful day for a vacationing lady—or gentleman. The gentlemen would walk a little farther and more lustily, swinging their canes, and some enjoyed a little fishing. We kids just let the lovely days roll over our heads. We had books to read and we could roam wherever and whenever we wanted. The arrival and departure of the train was a great event, and I was much impressed by the turning of the engine on the Y. And when Dad came out to join us it was a great thrill to gallop down the hill, greet him effusively and either walk back with him or ride up in the Inn's conveyance.

There was a Life Saving Station, and one of the few sources of entertainment offered by Montauk was to go to the Station, by carriage, and watch their life saving drill.

The Life Saving Service (which has since become the Coast Guard) was both exciting and boring. The whole Great South Beach was patrolled by these men who were trained and equipped to rescue seamen in distress. The stretch from Montauk Point to Fire Island Inlet was a noted hazard to shipping. Ships headed for New York would come in too close in order to cut the distance to port, or their navigation would fall short, and many a ship found itself caught on a sand bar, to hang there and pound to pieces in the surf.

The stations were five miles apart for 80 miles, from Montauk to the Fire Island Light at the inlet. Men patrolled in pairs on foot twenty-four hours a day, come hail, rain, sleet or snow. Each patrol made its two and a half miles, met its counterpart from the next station, and checked back to its respective headquarters by the phone that was the only sign of civilization on the beach—just a thin cobweb of single telephone wire on light-weight poles behind the dunes. Then two and a half miles back and another pair started out. I don't know how they signalled "ship in distress." There was always a man in the lookout tower atop the station and no doubt one of his duties was to watch for such signals. This foot patrol of the Great South Beach went right through the second World War.

Watching the life saving drill was very exciting. It was a matter of working against time and the elements to get the heavy surf boat out of the boat house and down the rollers to the water and then to launch it, no matter the condition of the surf. There was also breeches-buoy drill. For practice, the line was shot to a man on the "wreck pole." He fastened it, hauled up the breeches buoy, stepped into it, and was hauled back to safety. This was often used instead of the surf boat, and crewmen would be taken off a wrecked ship one by one.

It was grim and dangerous work when the surf ran high and a ship was slamming on the bar. In between times it was either boring or peaceful, depending on how a man looked at it. The Station was run with nautical precision, everything was immaculately clean, comforts were Spartan. There was as much chipping of paint and constant repainting as there was on a clipper ship caught in the doldrums.

The Station was supplied by the Service but the men added to these food

"South over the grass-covered knolls from Observatory Hill." The rolling downs at Montauk, 1898 *Courtesy of Suffolk County Historical Society*

stores. They fished. They would carry a big net out in one of the surf boats while men on the shore held one end. The boat would move in an arc and come back to shore farther down the beach. Then they would pull in the net, full of fish. They threw back the trash fish and either ate the good fish fresh or put them down in salt for winter use. The big skimmer clams came in on certain tides and they made a chowder to gladden a man's heart, or clam fritters to both gladden his heart and sit heavy on his stomach. In the fall the migrating ducks and geese added to the menu.

The second wild diversion at Montauk was riding out to the Lighthouse. This must have been at least five miles from the village and the Inn. We rode in a surrey—complete with fringe—and fought mosquitoes all the way, especially in the low spots where it was windless and boggy. But here you found those blueberries, and the fragrant azalea in season. The mosquitoes were just an accepted nuisance.

The Lighthouse stood isolated on its cliff at the tip of the Island. In fact, it still stands there looking just the same. In its isolation it is as exciting and fascinating as Land's End in England.

This was the first lighthouse built in the United States and was commissioned by George Washington in 1795. It was built of fieldstone and concrete and the walls at the base are eight feet thick. When it was built it stood 297 feet back from the edge of the cliff but as of 1970 there were only 49 feet left.

The whole thing is an automated marvel now, but when we went out there in the surrey Captain Scott was the Keeper. He was not a young man but was still able to climb up and down the narrow spiral stairs and tend the big kerosene lamps

The lighthouse at Montauk Point in the early 1900s

that sent their magnified light through the revolving prisms in their assigned code of flashes. The heavy glass that surrounded this tower room was pitted and pockmarked by the beaks of birds that had hit it, dazzled by the light, and had gone to their deaths below. We climbed the light more than once and left our names in the visitors' book in the nautically immaculate room below.

There may have been a Mrs. Scott although I think that the Captain "did for himself" at the time we knew him. A man would have to be of the stuff of hermits to live with a lighthouse but there were those who loved it and wanted no other way of life.

After a trip to the Point we watched the flashing light with proprietary interest. Back home we could see the flashes from the Fire Island Light projected high in the sky on a hazy night and this light I have also climbed.

One could visit the fishing village and when the boats came in it was a busy, if slightly fishy, place. The fish were cleaned, iced, and packed into cars for the LIRR to rush to the city market.

The Conklin House was a typical summer hotel with the summer flavor of straw matting and wooden walls that were made of some kind of vertical paneling, well-varnished. They never used plaster in these hotels and of course it was before the days of wallboard. The main room was large and airy with a huge stone fireplace. The usual veranda went around three sides of the house and you could find a rocker on the sunny side or the shady side, as you wished.

Mrs. Conklin ran the establishment. She was a dear, sweet, plump person with gray hair. Captain Conklin skippered one of the fishing boats and kept the

The Conklin House, the original "Old Inn" at Montauk,
1922   *Photograph by EFF*

Inn supplied with fish and lobsters. There was a big cat named Blackie who was
a friend of mine.

In time, Carl Fisher undertook to develop Montauk as he had developed
Miami Beach. That monstrosity of a little skyscraper went up and the dear old
Conklin House was torn down to make way for Montauk Manor. Golf courses
were laid out and Fort Pond Bay became a yacht basin. A few bits of acreage were
sold and elegant summer places were built by those who could afford them. Then
came the 1929 crash and the development of Montauk fell apart.

A friend once pointed out to me what he called the "Old Inn." Montauk
Manor the Old Inn! Only the old Conklin House standing on that same hill with
the downs sweeping quietly around it could be called the Old Inn.

The William C. Fergusons of Flushing and Garden City, who would one day
be my in-laws, also stayed at the Conklin House and Mr. F. ranged far and wide
on botanizing expeditions. Our two families never met. A twenty-one-year-old
Donald would never have looked twice at a twelve-year-old me—he probably
wouldn't have looked once. But the mills of the gods were grinding.

Gardiner's Bay was on the north side of the point and on the south side there
was a great crescent of ocean beach called Singing Beach. It was all rocks and gravel
that rolled when the waves washed in and out. They did indeed sing. Don told of
the day when he went for a swim just west of this beach.

This was back in the days of his brash young manhood, when he was a
swimmer par excellence. His idea of a swim was to take off due south, straight out
to sea, fool around for an hour or so, and then swim back in. Unfortunately, on
this day he got into an offshore current that was sweeping around the Point. I don't
know how long it took him but it did take every ounce of strength and endurance
to work his way out of the current and get back in. The people on the beach who
had watched him go out—and nobody overlooked Don in his heyday for he was
six feet three of bone and muscle and as handsome as need be—were about to alert
the Life Saving Service when he arose dripping from the sea. I hope they smothered
him with all their towels for he says he shivered for hours.

Donald Ferguson, long-distance swimmer, 1920   *Photograph by Edith V.D.
Ferguson*

The wide-open spaces at Montauk were often used as a location site by the New York movie companies. We saw the famous Annette Kellerman who was starring in a film—silent, of course—called *Neptune's Daughter*. They made this on and around Gardiner's Island and the crew and cast stayed at the Conklin House. We were there with Mother for one of her rare vacations and we were much impressed by the glamour and excitement of the stars, director, and cameramen with their caps back-to-front. They went off to Gardiner's Island each day to do the shooting so we didn't really see much but we were able to watch one scene that was shot near the Inn. I have no idea how it fitted into the plot, or even what the plot was, but the scene consisted of one witch-like actress poking her head through the branches of a windswept tree and cackling, "Ha, ha!" Of course this was done over and over until the director got a satisfactory take.

We missed by two weeks another company doing scenes for *Under Two Flags* with Theda Bara. Now, that I would have liked to see. It would have been well worth watching, with the Arabs charging in across the Montauk desert, and who-knows-what dramatic goings-on.

Dad had seen a lot of Montauk when it was the Isolation Camp for troops returning from Cuba at the end of the Spanish American War. These boys coming back from Cuba and the epic of San Juan Hill brought yellow fever with them so they were bivouacked on the Montauk downs until the epidemic ended.

All this was before my time but through my youth I remember Dad feeling affronted because the Army wouldn't take him. I can't imagine why, and I have a strong feeling he never tried, for that was in 1898, the year he and Mother were married. In fact, it was on June 3, their wedding day, that Admiral Hobson made his choice and sank his ship to block the harbor at Santiago.

"Bunkies." Rough Riders encamped at Montauk, 1898   *Courtesy of Suffolk County Historical Society*

I am sure it was the Rough Riders who took Dad's fancy. They were a volunteer cavalry regiment of cowboys and other rugged outdoorsmen who had been recruited by Lt. Col. Theodore Roosevelt and were under the command of Col. Leonard Wood. Their doings must have brought back Dad's boyhood memory of Custer and his men riding hell-for-leather through Cincinnati. I doubt that he was enough of a horseman for the cavalry and I am sure Mother had other ideas and went quietly on with her wedding dress. So Dad cheered for Col. Teddy at San Juan Hill and for Dewey at Manila and spent a lot of time at Montauk taking pictures of the troops.

"A double hold-up. Good guns in bad hands." This *Puck* cartoon takes aim at food speculators, c.1906.

Home Hampers: Farm to Family—Fresh

Dad was infuriated at the way fruits and vegetables left the farms beautifully grown and ripe for eating, and then were rattled by train to the city, tossed around in the Produce Market, sold to the retailer, rattled back and out to Garden City or Patchogue or Huntington, handled and rehandled in the store, and finally found their way to the dining table. The fact that each handler took his cut and thereby raised the ultimate price also enraged him. In our youth the Commission Merchants were visualized as demons of the first order.

In the *Agronomist* we have a light-hearted but slightly cynical paragraph in Dad's decidedly complex language:

> *Comic Opera Season.* Opened the middle of April. Leading characters by the Perennial Fruit Speculators, Supernumerary Good Things, the Orchardists, Supernumerary Easy Money, the City Consumers; same old opening chorus handed out by the speculators' merry press agents to the consumers' sources of universal knowledge, "peach crop ruined," with variations to get the consumers prepared for extortionate charges. Press notices revamped and ready for later publication in orchardists' sources of universal knowledge, "Bumper crop of peaches, markets glutted," also with variations to fully prepare the orchardist that he may gratefully accept financial returns almost covering the cost of the shipping baskets. Closing of the season chorus by the select specs: "The fruits of earth are ours for keeps; we buy for little but sell for heaps. Going and coming is all the same, producers and consumers are easy game."

Oh, they were really the bad guys.

We were still at Wading River when Dad conceived the idea of the Home Hamper with the slogan "Farm to Family—Fresh." All produce was picked and packed one day and the hampers were dispatched by Railway Express at the crack of dawn the next so they would reach their destination that same day, often by noon.

The hamper was a crate that held six four-quart baskets: three on the bottom, a divider, and three more on top. I spent hours, as did everyone else, on the packing of these hampers and I never missed the early morning trip to the station to attach the waybills and get them aboard the six o'clock train. I can still remember the smell of sweetfern and oak on those dewy mornings and I can still see the mist in the hollows that would be dispersed by the sun before we got back home. This was at Medford when we had grown big enough to be a part of the work force. Two days a week were Home Hamper days and the whole Farm turned to and joined the ratrace.

Ratrace? There was no ratrace in 1912! We all worked hard and kept at it but there was no danger of anybody having a nervous breakdown. Dad might steam around but that's the way he functioned and I don't remember him doing much of the packing. I think Mother was really in charge of packing. Dad had worked out a packing shed that ran the full length of the pumphouse. A huge zinc-lined sink with spray-nosed faucets and zinc-covered wings on each side facilitated the washing. We worked here back-to-back with those working at the packing table that also ran the full length of the shed.

Peas and strawberries are featured in an early-season Home Hamper.

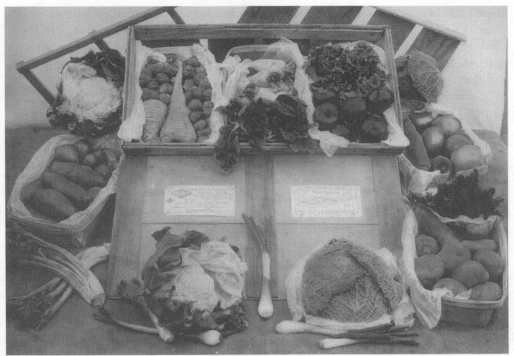

A late-season Home Hamper holds tomatoes, root vegetables and brussels sprouts.

Each member of the Farm force had an assigned job. Everything was picked that morning. Squash, peppers, and eggplant came in quickly but peas and beans took time. The fruit had to be handled carefully and chosen a touch on the firm side for even the tender care accorded to Home Hamper produce could bruise a dead-ripe peach. Little new-dug potatoes were scrubbed; beets and carrots, radishes or little turnips were cleaned, topped, and bunched. Asparagus was cut, sorted, bunched, and tied with raffia.

Each basket was lined with waxed green paper that folded over the top and kept peas from escaping and held in moisture and freshness. A basket might hold a combination of goodies. A head of lettuce, a bunch of radishes and a bunch of scallions would make a salad right there; an eggplant and several peppers made a nice color combination besides whetting the appetite; carrots and beets fitted together and a full box of well-cleaned spinach in its fresh dark green curliness was a pretty sight. Fruit went on top, carefully packed so nothing would shift in transit. Japanese plums made a lovely basket, or two quarts of strawberries, or three pints of raspberries. The raspberry pack that Dad fancied was one pint of reds, one of blacks or purples and one of yellows. Corn just went in between two boxes and was usually Golden Bantam.

All of this would have gone smoothly and easily if it weren't for the people who wanted changes. Mrs. T. might hate string beans so we'd have to find a substitute; Mrs. Y's family might simply adore eggplant but disdain squash so her hamper had to be packed accordingly. I think it was Hope who kept track of these odd hampers and saw to it that Mrs. Y. got her extra eggplant and Mrs. T. got Swiss chard instead of beans. By nightfall, they were all packed and the covers nailed on, and they were labeled.

They had to be at the station two miles away, ready to load on the six o'clock train, so it made for an early start. I wonder how long it took to make that two-mile trip in a farm wagon—speedier in the IHC of course, when it appeared. Time meant very little to me, and somebody else worked out the timetable.

What I liked, and what made me feel very important, was sorting out the waybills and getting the right one on each hamper. The station agent would have made out these waybills the day before and he left them out for us along with the pot of glue and the wide brush. I sorted them and somebody else swiped the glue under and over them.

In early spring, late fall, and even through the winter, hampers were packed with lettuce, radishes and scallions from the hotbeds, and potatoes, parsnips and such from the root cellar. The *Agronomist* states in 1911 that they had to quit in February because they were "out of keepers and coldframe and hotbed fresh things." These coldframes and hotbeds ran the length of the cow barn with full exposure to the southern sun.

The Farm shipped hampers to all kinds of places and to all kinds of people. In July of 1908, according to the *Agronomist*, they shipped one to Paris and the

"Home Hamper demand exceeds supply. Appropriate pageant depicts regret."
Elliot Morton, Hope and Eleanor, 1909

request was mainly for sweet corn. The packing of this hamper posed some problems. A photo of it shows that Dad used much waxed green paper and wrapped each ear of corn in an open-ended tube of his photographic blotting paper. It left New York aboard the *Deutschland* in the "cool box" on July 23 and a letter of praise and enjoyment was written on August 3. At some subsequent time the same request came from England but it seems that the eating of corn on the cob posed a problem in etiquette for our English cousins. "It should be nibbled off the cob in the privacy of the family circle only," was their verdict. Now, what would they do with a wedge of watermelon?

One of these hampers cost $1.50, delivered by Railway Express in Brooklyn or New York. That is, up as far as 135th Street. Beyond this was hinterlands and the Express people washed their hands of it. This $1.50 was a most excellent price. Dad claimed that for the same quantity of produce the New Yorker would have to pay from $2 to $4 in the markets. He also stated that he made 96 cents more than he would have gotten if he had shipped to the commission houses.

When I think of the man-hours that went into the raising, harvesting and packing of these things I have an idea that labor costs can't have been considered at all. However, with farm help receiving from $30 to $50 a month (with board and lodging), or $1 to $2 a day for casual labor, it was not a large consideration. A foreman's pay, according to Dad, varied "stupendously," from $35 a month to $5000 a year. That board and lodging also varied stupendously. When you consider that a man worked a six-day week, or even a seven-day week where stock had to be cared for, and a twelve-hour day, he really earned his stupendously varying pay.

The Fergusons of Garden City were friends of Ralph Peters and heard about the railroad farm and Dad's attempt to get farm produce direct to the consumer, so hampers went regularly to Point O' Woods on Fire Island during the summer. It was a noted summer colony even then and the name appealed to me so I remember having seen it on the waybills. However, I have no recollection of the name Mrs. William C. Ferguson. Nor had I any way of knowing that it was often young Mr. Donald who met the boat and trundled the hamper to the Ferguson cottage on the ocean front.

Another small bypath on our road of Destiny.

Superintendent Potter's inspection train on the bridge over the Carmans River south of Yaphank, 1897 *From the collection of Ron Ziel*

We Were Railroad Children

Steam engines held—and still hold—a fascination. As a tourist attraction, a short ride behind a steam locomotive will draw fans from hundreds of miles. And rightly. They have personality.

Does your heart pound when you see a diesel engine plodding down the track? Do you long to go places when you hear its miserable whistle? Heavens, no! The diesel may accomplish the same purpose but completely without any touch of drama. A diesel may have an efficient whistle but it doesn't call to you and speak of far-away places and the excitement of following the rails. It merely announces that the 8:17 is late.

A steam locomotive not only had personality, it had power and beauty. Its deep, mellow whistle was a siren call, and its rolling plumes of smoke and steam were clouds of glory. The sounds of its stopping and its starting were the kinds of noises that a small boy liked to imitate.

To watch a train come into the station was like watching a command performance. The whistle in the distance proudly announced its approach and you would gaze down the track with joyous anticipation. And step back. The great black shining thing rolled past with the rods moving slower and slower and the steam wisping out in all sorts of odd places. Then it would come to a stop with a sigh, and stand quietly chuffing and puffing with perhaps a sharp release of steam from the steam dome.

At a signal from the Conductor, the Engineer would throw his levers and nudge his monster back into motion. "Chuff! Chuff! Chuff!" and perhaps a rattling "chuff!" if the wheels slipped on wet or icy rails. The rods would start their back-and-forth movement as the big drivewheels turned, the Fireman might swing the bell, smoke and steam poured out, and gradually it would be off and away.

We were true railroad children. We loved trains passionately and a steam engine was as gorgeous to us as was ever a knight's great charger to a child of the Middle Ages. By extension, the men who drove, maneuvered, and cared for these gorgeous behemoths were heroes, and they knew it. The Engineer sat his cab in blue and white striped overalls, blue and white striped cap, and red bandanna around his neck with as much pride as that ancient knight sat his charger. If the stop was long enough—a heavy load of express to be put aboard, perhaps—he might dismount and go around his steed with a long-spouted oilcan and touch certain crucial spots with a squirt of oil. In his other hand was always a hunk of cotton waste for tenderly wiping off any excess.

We just liked trains wherever or whenever we saw them. We always checked the freight cars for the names of their railroads. It was like a tour of the USA. Boston and Maine; Union Pacific; Delaware, Lackawanna and Western—they all traveled together companionably. Many had nicknames that Dad taught us but the only one I remember is the DL&W which was known as the Delay, Linger and Wait. Of course our fierce loyalty to the LIRR made it the choicest railroad in the land. The Pennsy came next for that was the parent railroad.

Not a train went by the Farm that we kids didn't check through—the farthest sound of a whistle brought us running to stand in the road and wave to the Engineer. And the most important to see through was Charlie Beach's train that went west at 6 a.m. and back east to Riverhead at 8 p.m. Charlie Beach was the Engineer of the train that carried away the Home Hampers. And Charlie Beach was one of the highlights of our lives.

In the summer we would fall out of bed and into enough clothes to be presentable and tear out to the road where he could see us—usually all three of us—in a wildly waving row. And he would not only wave back, he would blow the whistle to us. He was the only one who did that—but then he was *ours*.

In the winter when the days shortened at each end, we still saluted him morning and night by blinking the lights to him. Dad was always up by six, and we were all around at eight p.m., so the front porch light was flicked off and on and he replied with his whistle. Christmas was wild—*everybody* was up and *every* light in the house was snapped on and off for as long as he could see them, and he just leaned on the whistle and blew it halfway to Medford. The Fireman may have taken a dim view of this or he may have worked up an extra head of steam in anticipation of this ritual. The return trip that night got the same treatment.

He came to see us one Sunday, driving a steamer—naturally. It was not a Stanley Steamer, but a White. He brought Mrs. Charlie Beach with him and it was like having Santa and Mrs. Claus sitting at your very own dining table. Another day he stopped at the Farm to pick up passengers and his engine failed him. He couldn't start it up again, so they had to send for help. I have no idea who, or what kind of help—maybe another engine from the Ronkonkoma yards. But *he* came down to the house and had breakfast with us. At that time, Loring had a

Engineer Charlie Beach

locomotive of his own—one he sat in and propelled by means of pedals, but it looked real. He was thrilled when Charlie Beach checked it out and admired it.

Even though the Engineer was at the throttles, the Conductor was Captain of the ship. The Conductor in his navy blue uniform snapped his fat pocket watch open and shut and clicked his ticket punch with authority. He had two henchmen under him, the Trainman and the Brakeman. They all wore the blue uniform, and each man's cap bore the appropriate title. All three worked at picking up and punching tickets or graciously acknowledging passes. Each ticket punch had a different pattern and we liked to collect the small bits of punched-out paper.

The Conductor and the Engineer communicated by a system of signals, the Conductor with a signal cord that ran the length of the train and the Engineer with his whistle. The Farm was a whistle stop. After the train left the station at Medford—or Yaphank if it was westbound—the Conductor, upon request, would give his signal cord three yanks. Dad said that this meant "Stop next station," to which the Engineer replied with three toots on the whistle, "Yes I will."

If, on the other hand, you wanted the train to stop and pick you up, you put out a green and yellow flag. At the end of the path from the house, close to the track, there was a post with a wooden compartment on the front. This held the flag, rolled around its stick, when it was not in use. When the flag was needed, it was removed from the compartment, unrolled, and its stick put into a hole in the front of the post so that it hung out at an angle. Of course you had to take down the flag, roll it up, and return it to the compartment before you leaped onto the train.

We traveled now and then from Medford to the Farm in the caboose of a freight train. This was most exciting if we could go up and sit in the lookout on top of the caboose.

"First rotary snowplow used east of the Rocky Mountains clearing LIRR tracks"

We each had an annual pass on the Long Island and Dad had annuals on most of the country's roads. The rest of us could always get a trip pass simply by writing for it. So we got around. We often traveled by parlor car, although there was a small charge for this. They were elegant and comfortable cars with a fat, upholstered chair for each passenger that swiveled at will so you could look out the window or converse with your neighbor, or even with the neighbor across the aisle. Each car had its porter to serve you. Gentlemen's coats and hats were whisked away in his care to be brushed and returned at the end of the run.

On long trips it was Pullman travel and this again was comfortable and with the service of a porter to each car. The making up of berths at night was fascinating as seats turned into beds. Getting undressed and dressed again in the morning made for some gymnastics. The porter moved his ladder as needed for us spry ones who slept in the upper berths.

There was one drawback to traveling behind a steam engine—cinders. Those gorgeous plumes of smoke carried quantities of fine cinders that infiltrated the cars—even the plushy parlor cars and elegant Pullmans. There were always drifts of them on the window sills. The plush seats were gritty, and the gloves, which all ladies wore when traveling, were in need of washing at the end of a train trip. Only a fool would wear white or light-colored gloves. It was worse in summer when windows were opened.

Eating in the dining car was great fun. It made a break in a long day, for one thing. Walking through swaying car after swaying car was an expedition but then you came to the dining car with its crisp white tablecloths, its shining water carafes, its amiable waiters and the dignified head waiter who seated you and flourished a great menu in front of you. I don't remember what we ate except for dessert. This was usually vanilla ice cream and I was always interested in the fact that the ever-present cinders had managed to get into it. This didn't bother me. I ate it with relish. Years later, I discovered that when you use the vanilla bean for flavoring you get the tiny black specks of seeds in the ice cream.

In the summer of 1914, Mother and we three kids went to Michigan for a vacation. This I remember well. We stayed in Petosky. We went out on small side trips, and one was to a lumber camp. It was my first look at big woods. What impressed me most was the gorgeous white cedar growing along the lake front. This I knew as arbor vitae.

We also went out to a nearby spot where the local Ojibwa Indians enacted Longfellow's "Hiawatha." The audience was seated on the lake shore and the stage was a small island with the whole of Lake Michigan in the background. I knew "Hiawatha" well enough to be at home with it, and when Hiawatha departed into the sunset, standing upright and paddleless in his canoe, I was duly thrilled. The next day we were walking along the shore and came upon the gear that had pulled his canoe into the sunset, but even that didn't spoil the romantic tale for me.

We saw Niagara Falls and the Gorge, Luray Caverns and Natural Bridge, Florida and Colorado, among other places, thanks to the LIRR and the passes. I traveled to and from school on Cape Cod for five years by pass. Later I went back and forth to school at Ambler the same way and we went many times to Bristol and to West Chester, Pennsylvania.

It was a real blow when I was married and had to buy a ticket in order to ride on the LIRR, but my loyalty remains true. When an unkind word is spoken of the LIRR, it is spoken about the railroad that I love.

"Motive power before the day of tractors"

Eureka Farm—My Heart's Home

The trips to West Chester, Pennsylvania were the supreme joy of my youth. The Walters lived there at Eureka Farm. Aunt Anna was my mother's dearest friend and had been her bridesmaid. As Mother loved the family, so did we. I had a special love for them. Either I was born fifty years too late or I had already spent a reincarnation on such a farm, for when I was at West Chester I was home—I belonged. I was in the niche the Lord meant for me.

Grandpa Walter was the owner and operator of Eureka Farm. I never knew Grandma Walter. She died before my time. There was Aunt Anna, and Aunt Leonore, and Uncle Horace—all unmarried, and all part of the organization.

Uncle Horace had fallen downstairs as a baby and as a result he could not move his arms freely. His job was the feeding of the stock and they had all kinds of animals. There was always a young boy from the orphans' home to help him. It was he who took the produce into West Chester and delivered it on a door-to-door route. They had regular customers for the eggs and butter, chickens and apples or whatever was on hand at the moment. The boy went along but it was Uncle Horace who drove the "Democrat"—a horse-drawn wagon that looked much like the Amish vehicles.

Aunt Anna drove the "brake cart" with her own horse, Dunbar, a lovely brown horse with a dark stripe down his back. She sat straight and tall as a lady should and handled the reins as if she enjoyed it. The cart had two two-man seats, back-to-back, and half of the back one lifted up so you could get into the front. The only way in was from the rear.

Aunt Anna was my favorite. She was very erect, very thin and very full of fun. She was the housekeeper and had charge of the butter making and the young poultry. When I was there in the early spring I went down with her every day to the incubator room in the cellar and watched her turn each egg, put more kerosene in the smelly incubator heater, and check everything. I was there one spring when she had an incubator full of duck eggs. I loved baby ducks and thought it would be great fun to watch them hatch. Alas! They hatched the very day we had to leave and all I saw was a few eggs cracking and moving around as the small inmates prepared to meet the world. Aunt Leonore was the younger, and a different sort of person, quite like my mother—quiet and pretty and sweet. She was the office force and lady-in-waiting to that autocrat, Grandpa Walter. It can't have been easy. Nobody ever dared to disagree, or question his edicts, or suggest another way of doing something. He would have roared, and I am sure they had learned years before that Papa was undeniably in charge.

Both aunts spent much time on the housework, and Mary Reed was hard at it from daylight to dark. She was always called that—Mary Reed. She was a grand person. She was a black woman who had come from the orphans' home at an early age to be brought up by Grandma Walter and to help with the housework. I don't know what schooling she had but she was well-read and well-spoken. She may have been a servant (remember—one knew one's place in those days) but she was also a well-loved companion and the three women of the household worked together in perfect unison. We loved her and she was endlessly good to us kids.

Aunt Anna had had a blighted romance. She had been in love with a young man who was a traveling salesman. Her parents had vetoed the marriage so, true to her Victorian upbringing, Anna settled down to spend her days keeping house for her family. Aunt Leonore had an even more tragic blighted romance. She had been engaged to a neighboring young farmer when he came down with tuberculosis, that dreaded disease that once took so many lives. I think I remember him—or the fact that he was dying on a nearby farm.

This was a very different kind of farm from ours. They were self-sufficient, as any farm family was, but they also raised field seed for sale—their Dent corn, which was quite famous, and other grain seed. They sold livestock—mainly pigs, I think, but also cows, and probably sheep. I remember all kinds of creatures—big farm horses, driving horses, cows, sheep, pigs, chickens, ducks and guinea fowl, and the dogs.

The dogs belonged to Aunt Leonore. She raised collies—that is, she did the paper work. Uncle Horace and his young helper did all the rest. Not that it was arduous. They were farm-raised dogs so they had the run of the farm, except when one was having puppies. Should one need to be confined, a spot could be found in the sheep pen or the feed house, so puppies might be found anywhere.

I don't think there were any bloodlines involved in breeding these dogs. It was intelligence and stamina that counted and a good dog stood on his own merits. It was when the world became enamored of Albert Payson Terhune and his Lad of Sunnybank that the breed and breeding changed. I never could become so attached to the long-nosed breed that replaced the border-type collies they originally raised. Of the long-nosed crew, I remember Junior particularly. He was

Grandpa Walter, the patriarch of Eureka Farm in West Chester, Pennsylvania

a sweet and rather bumbling dog and inclined to get into trouble—like coming up on the front porch. At such a breach of etiquette, Grandpa Walter would roar and thump his cane and Junior would flee. Perforce I would follow him and comfort him.

The dogs' food was cooked in huge kettles just inside the kitchen door. These must have been set up for some other purpose originally—for the making of apple butter or scrapple, I would guess. Two enormous black pots were set in form-fitting holes in a construction of yellow brick. Below was the fire which was stoked with wood from an opening in the front. The dog food was a concoction of meat scraps and cornmeal ground from their own corn. This was stirred with heavy poles and it heaved and bubbled like a seething volcano or the mud puddles at Yellowstone Park. It would not be considered an ideal dog diet these days but vitamins had yet to be invented.

I first became acquainted with Pennsylvania wildflowers at West Chester. They were so different from the ones we have on Long Island. Instead of arbutus it was hepatica and bloodroot that poked up through the dry brown leaves in the woods. Spring beauty frothed along the edge of the woods, and May apples stood singly along the roadside with their green umbrellas shading the beautiful white blossoms. Forget-me-nots made blue ruffles along the edge of the brook at the foot of the meadow and watercress grew in the cold running water.

The big barn stood near the main road. The big hay wagons would roll in and the hay would be pitched up into the huge mows. I was never there at haying time but we had fun climbing and jumping in the hay, way up among the rafters. There

Sheep in the pasture at Eureka Farm

was a chute down which hay could be pitched to the lower levels where the cows and horses were stabled.

At one corner of the barn was the sheep pen, and squeezed in between barn and feed house, on a steep slope, was the garden. This was in the care of the ladies of the house and they had vegetables and a blaze of flowers all summer long. There was a farm bell on a pole at the top of the garden. It clanged lustily to call people to meals. We also had a bell at Medford and this was used more than once to rally forces to fight a forest fire.

The big old stone house stood under great old elm trees. The orchard and meadowland fell away from the house so you looked out over it all from the wide front porch. The pasture swept down the hill to a lovely brook at the foot. Beyond the brook there was a zigzag rail fence—a snake fence—and a huge cornfield that swept up the opposite hill. One beautiful elm tree stood in the pasture by the brook. It made a grateful patch of shade at noonday for sheep or cows—whichever was pastured there at the time. One of Dad's loveliest pictures was of sheep under this tree.

The porch was well used in summer. Besides the usual rocking chairs, they had a porch swing—a long seat suspended from the ceiling by chains. You got a slight forward-and-back movement not unlike that of a rocking chair. It was a pleasant seat to share with an aunt in the afternoon when they had an hour to relax between washing the dinner dishes and starting supper.

There was also a real swing suspended from the enormous elm that shaded the porch. I spent much time there. The swing took you forward into space, back over safely close ground, and then forward again with your feet miles in the air— or so it seemed. We might have likened it to flying if we had even thought of flying.

Not far from the swing and down a neat boardwalk was the outhouse— always used, winter and summer. A chilly adventure it could be. The last thing at night, we ladies made an expedition with lantern in hand if there was no moonlight to show the way.

At the side of the house was the orchard, with gnarled old apple and pear trees. They were great for climbing. Behind the orchard were the fowl houses with assorted fowl in residence. A wineberry bush grew along the chicken yard fence and I checked this a dozen times a day lest a berry achieve edible ripeness unbeknownst to me.

Below the orchard and at the edge of the big pasture was the pig house, very large and full of pigs of all sizes. Uncle Horace could call a pig with the best of them and, when he and his attendant boy opened the door and he let out his strident call, every snout in the place was lifted. He also called the cows. They wandered in across the meadow with their bells bonging. These bells were pleasant but their real purpose was to locate the herd if they wandered up into the woods.

The house was old. A great, solid, Pennsylvania stone house with walls three feet thick and three-foot-deep window sills to prove it. The two rooms used for living were the living room and the dining room. The two parlors across the hall were opened upon occasion but it had to be a real occasion.

The kitchen ran the full depth of the house. The floor was paved, rather unevenly, with red brick and slanted up from front to back so you spent the day walking uphill and downhill. There were three little steps up to the dining room that had to be navigated many times a day. The cooking operations were carried on at the uphill end with a large table, a kitchen cabinet and a great black coal-burning stove as equipment. At the end of the stove was a hot water reservoir made of copper, hence called "the copper." You dipped your hot water out as needed.

Almost the full length of the kitchen was used on washday. The three women heated water in quantity—in the big black kettles, I guess—and set up several washtubs on stands. One tub was for scrubbing—with a scrubbing board. One was for rinsing, one for bluing, one for starching. I don't remember whether they had wringers or not. In those days a lot of washing was done with nothing but two strong wrists to wring out the clothes. I started that way in the 1920s and then graduated to a hand-cranked clothes wringer that clamped to the edge of the tub and squeezed out the water between two rollers.

It was too bad if a woman didn't like housework in those days for it was a full-time job. Plumbing was nonexistent. Each bedroom had its full set of crockery. There was a big washbowl with a big pitcher standing in it and a small pitcher beside it. The small one was often used to carry up some hot water from the copper for shaving or brushing the teeth or for taking the chill off the cold water in the big pitcher. There was a toothbrush mug and a soap dish. The covered slop jar stood on the floor and the necessary chamber pot went behind closed doors below the big bowl. Many of these chamber sets were really beautiful, as lovely as table china.

Every morning the slop jar and the pot had to be emptied, downstairs and outside, and the crockery cleaned and the big pitcher refilled. Eventually they had a bathroom installed, which must have changed life entirely.

The guest room that we used had two beds—a double bed and a three-quarter one. The latter had a featherbed in the winter and we loved this. You climbed up on a chair, leaped and disappeared into the feathery softness. Wonderful on winter nights for there was no heat at all in the bedrooms.

The aunts worked together to make the beds. Making up a featherbed took skill. One aunt on each side shook it up and down and got the feathers redistributed and then smoothed it back into place. It was as fat and beautiful as a loaf of bread ready for the oven but we knew we would collapse it into feathery nests at bedtime.

There was a choice quilt on the big bed that was an endless delight to me. I think Grandma Walter made it. It was a patchwork quilt but made all of silk pieces. Each square was puffed over a tuft of wool, then these squares were stitched together, and each one was outlined with featherstitching. Aunt Leonore or Aunt Anna would go over it with me and tell me where each square came from—one was a dress of Mamma's, one a piece of Papa's necktie, another a favorite "best" dress. Brocades, plain satin, taffeta embroidered with tiny flowers—it was a marvel.

In the early days, the only heat was in the living room and the dining room, which also became the kitchen for the winter season. They put a stove in the middle of the living room and the fireplace burned constantly. They heaved the kitchen stove up the three steps into the dining room so they could shut off the brick-paved kitchen. This must have made things crowded, but certainly saved steps and energy.

Electricity eventually came, but in my early days of visiting it was oil lamps downstairs and candles in the bedrooms. There was a candlestand on the stair landing and we each took a candle to light ourselves to bed.

Uncle Horace smoked a pipe and he lighted it with spills. Making the spills was one of the small jobs that kept Aunt Anna from ever sitting idle. She taught us to make them. You cut newspapers into strips and rolled them in a certain way so you came up with what looked like a soda straw, but it was tight at one end and the top flared out into a little flag. You lighted this over a lamp and it served to ignite a pipe or a freshly laid fire. One didn't use matches carelessly. They cost money.

Cooking was no small job. Meals were hearty. Breakfast was a production. Of course, everyone had gotten a good start on the day's work by that time. Uncle Horace had fed at least some of his creatures and he came in ready for nourishment. One started with oatmeal and cream—that real farm cream. Then ham and eggs

Eureka Farm, West Chester, Pennsylvania.

and fried potatoes, or fried potatoes and creamed chipped beef, or even steak. Often it was their own scrapple or sausage. Toast and coffee, again rich with cream. After this, a man was ready to get on with the morning's work. Dinner at noon called for meat and potatoes and vegetables, side dishes of sauces and relishes and pickles, and pie or a baked pudding for dessert. I can't remember supper—something simple, maybe baked beans or hash.

They smoked their own meat, raised their own vegetables, gathered wild strawberries and anything else that was there for the taking, had eggs aplenty and the milk, cream, butter and potcheese that comes of raising cows. They canned in the summer for winter eating. They really canned, in tin cans. Mother tried their way but decided for her glass jars.

All these cans, as well as pickles, relishes, jams and jellies, were kept in the cellar, which was a perfect Gothic stronghold. It was well below ground with the same thick stone walls, and windowless. They had a second cellar called the vault. I don't know whether this was unique or a common arrangement. It was a small room dug a floor below and in the center of the cellar. A flight of stone steps led down to a huge thick door at the bottom. You went down with your lamp in one hand and the newly made butter, or whatever, in the other. It was pitch black dark with no hint of the outside world and it was stone cold winter and summer. I doubt that the temperature varied a degree from June to January. Hitchcock would have loved it.

Going in to West Chester was a real bit of diversion. One of the aunts would drive and do the shopping. Finding a parking space was no problem—you didn't park. I can still see Aunt Leonore pulling up her spirited horse in front of the grocery store. The white-aproned grocer would come trotting out, pass a respectful time of day, and take her order with pencil and pad. On to the drugstore and the same thing happened, and so around the shopping area. Then a return round and the orders were tucked away under the seat with a gracious acknowledgement of the transaction, and off we went clip-clopping toward the farm. I suppose you had to get out to try on a pair of shoes or match the ribbon for your Sunday hat, but otherwise it was curb service.

I well remember one time when we went in to town with Mary Reed. We walked. I don't know how far it was. A mile and a half, at least. The purpose of this expedition was to get to Hokey Pokeys. The Hokey Pokey man was a sidewalk salesman. He had his little handcart and moved around town so we had to look for him. Once we found him, Mary Reed bought us our luscious treat. They call them ice cream sandwiches now—two Nabisco-type wafers with a square of ice cream between. Delicious in themselves, most welcome after a hot and dusty walk, and much appreciated because it was our dear friend, Mary Reed, who bought them for us.

I went to West Chester always with much joy, and left with regret. The time I spent there has left an indelible mark on me.

Diversions in Simpler Times

I sometimes wonder how Mother took the drastic change from the pleasant small-town society of Huntington to life on the Farm at Medford, with no social life of any kind. In Huntington she had many friends and there were social gatherings of all sorts—"hen parties" during the day and groups of couples in the evening. At one time, someone set up a gymnastics class for the women. This I remember for they all had to make "gym suits." They consisted of bloomers and some kind of top and it all led to much giggling, even among the grown-up ladies. I'm sure Dad approved heartily. Anything to get the women out of those stifling long skirts.

In the early days at Medford there was Margie Hartman who was as eager for a friendly face as was Mother. Her husband was William P. Hartman, known as Hartie, who ran the office at the Farm. They had the little portable house at the east end of the Farm, the one that Badger later turned into his Badger Den. There were a few oak trees there of respectable size and Dad had chosen it as a pleasant setting for a home. Margie and Hartie came from Circleville, Ohio and a typical small-town life so I imagine Margie must have had some lonely times too. She and Mother were congenial and they sewed and embroidered together. Margie did endless white embroidery with satin-stitch flowers and eyelets and buttonhole-stitch scallops. She dressed smartly and I was terribly impressed by her big hats, each with the veil fastened tightly over it and snugged under her chin.

Hartie and Margie now and again took us kids to the movies in Patchogue. This was about the only wild diversion available so our carriage horse, Pomona, would be hitched to the cabriolet and off we would go at Pomona's snail pace. I have yet to find out just what kind of conveyance this really was. I know Dad called it the cabriolet just because he liked the sound of the word. It was a two-seated job with a top and side curtains. Maybe it was just a surrey without the fringe on top.

Certainly Pomona never qualified as a high-steppin' strutter. Since she refused to get out of a walk, it was not a thrilling six-mile ride but we felt we were in good company.

I don't remember any of the movies we saw in those early days. They were, of course, silent films and since there was no sound track the necessary mood music was provided by a piano in the pit. A nimble-fingered piano player watched the screen and poured his heart out in appropriate music to accompany the action. That was an art unto itself—movie piano music.

After the show we would go to Ginocchio's ice cream parlor at the corner of Main Street and Ocean Avenue, catty-corner from McBride's Drugstore which is still there, for a soda. A chocolate soda with vanilla ice cream was my choice, and still is. But I remember one evening when I came to grief with this confection. I had worn my boarding school "dress uniform"—white Norfolk jacket and skirt, white stockings and shoes—and I had added a pale blue necktie. I felt that I was indeed a credit to the party and I drew my chocolate soda to me with aplomb and grace. Whammo! The whole thing tipped over and poured into my white lap—straw, foam, chocolate syrup and all, with the vanilla ice cream sitting in the middle of it. My day was ruined. My life was ruined. Kind people removed the ice cream and mopped me up but I rode the six miles home behind the phlegmatic Pomona reeking of chocolate and vanilla.

Circus Day and the Fourth of July were the big breaks in the summer routine of the Farm. The circus was a tremendous event when I was young. Everybody went to the circus. Most towns had a certain empty field that was used once a year by the circus and it grew to hay and weeds the rest of the year. It was usually handy to the railroad station, for the circus traveled by train. Huntington Station was called Fairground in my youth so this same spot must have been used for firemen's fairs and such. The circus field at Patchogue was west, nearer Blue Point. I can still smell the trodden grass, the roasting peanuts, and the animals. I admired the elephants and acrobats, especially the beautiful ladies who hung by their teeth and waved butterfly wings back and forth. Since my teeth were a sore point—and I do mean sore, what with five years of assorted dentists trying to straighten them—I admired anyone with a set of choppers equal to that.

On the Fourth of July the family had target practice with the resident rifle. Mother was always the best shot. We always had fireworks in the evening and all the neighbors were invited to join us. After the Medford Grange was established, it usually had a float in the Fourth of July parade in Patchogue. This would be a gorgeous affair, bedded down on hay in the Farm wagon, and there would be arches wrapped in red, white and blue crepe paper, the three Graces all in starched white dresses, and heaven knows what else. Flowers, no doubt, and much oak and pine to conceal the mechanics.

I recall one year I was allotted a seat as Flora—or maybe it was Ceres, or Pomona. These three Graces loomed large in the ritual of the Grange and it was

The farm wagon at Medford

a great honor to be so named. Badger was there in a straw hat lavishly trimmed with the aforementioned red, white and blue crepe paper. I think he drove the team. Whatever his assigned position, he took it with verve and dash, for Badger was a good bit of a ham.

Halfway to Patchogue a thunderstorm struck, and by the time it cleared the whole float was a wreck. The hay was soggy, the starched dresses had melted, the crepe paper had been reduced to a pulp, and everything and everybody was streaked with its non-colorfast red, white and blue. The trimming on Badger's hat had run and his white hair and white beard were downright psychedelic.

I have a feeling we turned around and went home. I'm sure I regretted this for I loved a parade with its marching bands, rippling flags, and the whole-hearted cheering of the bystanders who were filled with patriotism and Fourth of July zeal.

Decoration Day also had its parade and, in my early days in Huntington, there were enough Civil War veterans to make it very real. They rode in the few automobiles that were then available. Everyone in town cut armloads of flowers from the early summer gardens and all the GAR graves in the cemeteries were tenderly decorated. There were always poppies and iris and peonies in abundance. These days they aren't even in bloom by Decoration Day (now called Memorial Day) and the Civil War has been relegated to the history books. I remember the ceremony in front of the little old library that still stands on Main Street in Huntington. The statue there of Nathan Hale came in for some attention too, even if he did date back to the Revolution. I liked to sit on the little cannon, which is still standing, to watch the doings.

There was a horse trough near the Nathan Hale monument. The horse trough was to the horse of my early years what the service station is to the car of today. In my mind's eye I can see many of them. There was one in Coram in conjunction with the town pump. This stood right in the middle of the crossroads where the Patchogue-Port Jefferson Road crosses Middle Country Road. The Coram Hotel stood on the northeast corner and I daresay the driver stopped in for his mug of beer while the horse guzzled the water in the trough. Eventually the pump and horse trough were removed as a menace to traffic.

Parades and circuses and movies, and even chocolate sodas, were enjoyed with an enthusiasm and zest that are gone from the world nowadays. These breaks in the rhythm of work came but seldom, so they meant more. Entertainment was not considered necessary in my youth—it was just an occasional thing, so it was more thoroughly enjoyed. Dad collapsed with mirth over Charlie Chaplin, young and old gasped with admiration at the circus performers, and a fine uprush of adrenalin ran along the streets when the flags went by on the Fourth of July.

The very attitude toward work was different. Work was not looked upon as an unfortunate necessity, with leisure time, shorter hours, retirement pay, and fringe benefits the only bright spots in the worker's world. Work was just a way of life, and this attitude went back, I am sure, to pioneer days when a man survived by the work of his hands and thrived only if he was a good and intelligent worker. There was much pride to be found in his accomplishments too, and that pride in work is the key to the whole thing. When a woman took pride in "setting a good table" or taking a fine cake to a church supper, she didn't mind slaving all day over a hot stove, and when a man could look out over his well-tended acres and bed down his well-fed animals in his staunch, clean, and well-provisioned barn at night, his pride and satisfaction made for a contented man.

A good crop makes for a contented farmer.

I freely admit that farming is not for everyone but to a farmer it is a good life, or it was before it became big business. A man worked by a rhythm—the rhythm of the day and the rhythm of the seasons—but there was constant change within these rhythms. The chores morning and night started and ended each day, but otherwise your work was seldom the same. You might find hoeing onions a little monotonous on Monday, but Tuesday there would be beans to pick, and on Wednesday you might start filling the silo, and so on. And under it all was the awareness of the seasons rolling around, so you planned which field to put into corn *next* year even as you cut the ensilage from this year's crop. Farmers may have developed arthritis and bent backs in the days of real farming but they seldom had ulcers or heart attacks.

In our early days at the Farm, a monthly party was organized for the double purpose of training in the social graces for Hope and me and for the entertainment of the countryside. A program was arranged—the current governess must have been responsible for this—of recitations, songs, and tableaux. We also had to participate in the preparation and serving of refreshments. This was Mother's department—the womanly arts of kitchen and drawing room. We made cupcakes and cookies, cocoa and fruit punch. This we served after the entertainment.

The audience consisted of the whole Farm entourage and all the neighbors near enough to come. They arrived by foot or by wagon, in squeaky shoes and best clothes. The women curled their hair for the occasion. The men and boys were weather-tanned, heavy-handed and ill at ease. We made contact with these folk just when the advent of the automobile was doing away with their isolation, and country people were beginning to blend in with the rest of the world. I know many of the young people who came to our parties went on to become businessmen, teachers, nurses, or just plain bigger and more successful farmers than their fathers.

We weren't aware of it at the time, but we did lead an isolated life on the Farm. We in the Homestead were of a different social status from the rest of Medford. While it was not emphasized in 1912 or 1914, there was such a thing as social structure. There were no barriers but class was a very real thing and "knowing one's place" was still real too. Dad tried to break this down by treating everyone "as a human being" but what he really achieved was a paternalism which accepted responsibility and concern for the welfare of not only those at the Farm but all of Medford too. He became the equivalent of the Squire up at the Manor and we were gentry. This life we led in the early days certainly prepared me to welcome the English novel when I met it. It seemed so perfectly natural to me when all the villagers and the estate people were bid to the Christmas party at the Manor House.

Ah, Christmas! Everybody came to see the Christmas tree, and there were boxes and cornucopias of hard candy hanging on the branches for one and all. Frau Bolz came and cooked the Christmas dinner, which brings to mind the folks who lived south of the track.

Not that south was the wrong side of the track—just that that's where they lived. These people had had a rough deal. An unscrupulous developer by the name of Schwenke had acquired a vast acreage and sold lots to city people longing to move to the country. This land was sold sight unseen but with brilliant tales of its beauties and the possibilities for being self-sufficient on one's own land. A water system was to supply them all with water, and a factory had been erected where sweaters were to be manufactured, thus providing work to eke out the farm living.

When these poor souls moved out from the city, bag and baggage, they found that their land was nothing but burned-over scrub oak and pitch pine, the water system consisted of a very shaky tower holding no water, and the sweater factory was but a skeleton building with a skeleton sweater business. It was an outrageous situation but was typical of that age of the rapacity of the "haves" and the naive gullibility of the "have nots." Of course Dad had shown that this land could produce prodigious crops, but he had advantages not available to the small farmer—the manure that came from the Railway Express stables by the carload, and the Railroad treasury that paid the bills.

Gus and Lena Bolz had a pathetic place about a mile south of the Farm. Dad gave Gus a job working with the dairy herd and the crops. He was small and thin and had a drooping mustache, but what a transformation when he came to the monthly party. He wore a dashing, if slightly shabby, suit and a brown derby hat and the droopy mustache was transformed by mustache wax and tender care into a gorgeous Kaiser Wilhelm production, curled up as stiff as one of his cows' horns.

His wife helped Mother around the house on an odd-job basis. She was as hugely fat as Gus was thin. Her feet were enormous and must have been as flat as barges. She wore men's shoes with elastic sides and I know every step hurt. She was a dandy cook and made the best red cabbage. A Christmas dinner of her production was a real treat.

With his usual respect, Dad called her Frau Bolz, not Lena, and so we all knew her. She was so good to us kids, and devoted to Mother. She gave me a garnet necklace for a wedding present. I'm sure this was the only pretty thing she ever owned. I have the garnets still—unstrung and unworn for many years, but I treasure them. They were a real gesture of love. Like the Little Drummer Boy with the gift of his drumming, she gave me the only thing she had. I do hope she has found rest for her heavy body and her poor feet in the Hereafter.

To get back to Christmas, it really started months before the calendar ever intimated that it was imminent. We made all of our presents and at that time everybody, even unto the remotest cousin, had to have a present. In time, Hope took this over and spent the summer wrapping up pincushions and pen wipers and sachets. I suppose we all had a hand in the making, and I can still smell the violet and lavender sachet powder. But Hope wrapped and marked them and stored them away in a drawer of the bureau in the upstairs hall. This was the same bureau in which Dad laid the pears to ripen. One drawer was lined with an old wool blanket

The "pung," the farm wagon transformed into a sleigh. Passengers include Eleanor, Loring, ELF and Grandma Busy. c.1911

and the Seckels and Bartletts were laid there to mellow. That's the way his grandmother did it.

I don't really remember any of the Christmas presents that I made except for the first knitting I ever did, many long sweaters ago. This was a green sweater that I made for Mother the second year I was away at boarding school. This creation started large and got larger. I kept running out of wool, and every new ball I got was a slightly different shade of green, so it had a rather dissipated look by the time it was finished. But, undaunted, I put a row of gray angora around the collar and cuffs. It must have been some that Mother had at home, for she was great on angora wool for baby things. (Not really practical, for dribbled-on angora looks like a wet cat.) I presented it to her with bursting pride. She received it with astonishment, and wore it while I was at home. She must have laid it aside when I went back to school, and eventually she gave it to Frau Bolz. If it fit her mammoth figure I can imagine how Mother swam in it. I do know that Frau Bolz was enchanted with it and not only because it was warm but because I had made it. We were very good friends.

Dad went haywire at Christmas and must have blown the family resources in one grand spree. He loved to give, and nothing was too good for us, especially Mother. There were books and books, and all manner of pretty things. One year I had a lavender corduroy bathrobe with slippers to match, which made me feel like

The fireplace at Medford

a Crown Princess. One year Mother had a beautiful gold silk crepe robe—it would be called a housecoat these days—and she had beaded, bronze kid slippers to wear with it. It was our great delight to borrow these slippers on occasion. They had baby Louis XIV heels and we felt terribly elegant. A whole generation later my children wore these shoes and pretended to be Dorothy walking around Oz in witch's shoes.

The filling of the candy boxes was the beginning of the Christmas excitement. Besides the glossy hard candy, there were those satiny little pillows filled with a nutty-creamy concoction, and an occasional portly chocolate cream. It was a fearful temptation to eliminate these—they could hardly be classed as hard candies and there were so few that one usually put only one or two in a box—but the Golden Rule prevailed and we ate no more than our just share.

The Christmas tree was, of course, a pitch pine and this was very little trouble at Medford for we lived among pitch pines. I don't remember the getting of the tree but I well remember it filling the whole north end of the living room. Dad never would have settled for a small tree, or even a medium-sized tree, any more than my children or grandchildren would, and we had decorations enough for the Rockefeller Center tree. Not that there was a Rockefeller Center tree in those days. There was no Rockefeller Center.

When the tree was man-handled in and the house filled with that lovely piney smell, the excitement grew intense. We trimmed it on Christmas Eve. We had lovely ornaments. They were made in Germany in those days and were beautiful. Birds with spun glass tails, tiny balls in tinsel netting, miles of thick tinsel ropes and electric lights. I never knew Christmas tree candles, which must have been lovely, but what a danger.

The lights were in varicolored, many-sided lanterns that folded flat for storage. I don't know what the material was, isinglass I suppose. It was a heavy, ribbed, translucent substance that glowed like stained glass when the lights were turned on. Electric lights of any sort were impressive enough to the neighborhood but this tree with its colored lanterns was a great sight. And each one who came went home with one of the boxes or cornucopias of candy. Ah, the Manor was very gracious.

The hanging of the stockings was a ritual of tremendous import. This started several weeks before Christmas when we wrote our letters to Santa Claus. Everyone wrote, even Dad and Mother, expressing our heart's desires. I remember how overcome I was at the thought of one little fat man spending his days in granting the wishes of such as I, and my letter always included my heartfelt thanks for last year's largesse. I think I usually felt guilty at not writing sooner but we only had access to Santa Claus at Christmas time. We "mailed" our letters in the powderhorn that hung by the fireplace and one morning they would be gone and there might be an ashy footprint on the hearth to show that he had been there.

On Christmas Eve Dad hung the stockings. We each produced our own, and there was always one for the current dog and cat. After all, they were part of the family. The last thing before we went to bed we set out a snack for Santa—cider and crullers, or cookies and milk. And sometimes I added another note thanking him in advance for the treasures I knew I would find in my stocking. One year I also left him a present. This was the year Mother was punching brass. She always had some kind of handwork going and punched brass was in that year. I did a picture frame for Santa and made a picture to fill it. This was probably a pine tree in the snow and even that would have taxed my artistic ability to the limit. Anyway, I put my whole heart in it.

And so to bed—but not to sleep. There were tremendously exciting rustlings and thumpings from downstairs, and Mother's and Dad's murmurous voices, but finally we would fall asleep.

The hour for arising was pre-set. We had to be up and at our stations by six a.m. when Charlie Beach whistled his way past the Farm. I am sure we were awake by four o'clock at least and lay there in an agony of anticipation until it was time to get up. "Merry Christmas!" rang through the house and we repeated it and repeated it with wild excitement. The day had at long, long last arrived.

The ceremony of exchanging greetings with Charlie Beach accomplished, we went downstairs, still in nightgowns and robes, in solemn procession. The youngest went first, and so on up to Dad who brought up the rear, quite as thrilled with it all as any of us kids. Under the tree was a vast array of packages, but these we had to ignore for the time being.

The immediate business at hand was the stockings. Santa Claus had indeed been there for they bulged with many strange lumps and bumps. An andiron had been knocked over and ashes were strewn on the hearth; the cider had been drunk and only crumbs were left of the crullers. My gift was gone and I was overwhelmed by the thought that even now it might be on Santa's own mantel. I could even visualize Mrs. Claus looking at it over her glasses and saying, "Hmph—a nice child, no doubt, but not much of an artist." Being a naive child of a naive generation, I included Santa Claus—the actual, big-hearted, white-bearded gentleman—among my acquaintances to a very advanced age. Fortunately, I had learned that he was only a lovely myth before I found the punched brass picture frame up in the attic.

When each stocking had been emptied, from the candy cane in the top to the tangerine in the toe, we had breakfast, and then came the tree. With all the interfamily exchange of gifts, and with all the boxes from various cousins and aunts and uncles, it was a long and exhausting process. The latter part of Christmas Day is either a blur or a blank to me. I think I just picked out the choicest book and retired to consume it immediately. I am sure we collapsed into bed that night as soon as we had given Charlie Beach his evening salute.

Christmas was really a surfeit of riches and I'm afraid we have carried that tendency through to this day. The joy of giving carries you away and everyone goes a little mad. I say the joy of giving advisedly. Before Christmas, the thought of what you will get may loom largest in the conversation, but I have noticed that the greatest joy when the day comes is in watching someone open the gift you have chosen with much love and a desire to please. That is why I saw to it that my own children gave Christmas presents from the time they could first hold a pair of blunt-nosed scissors and hack pictures out of old magazines. These first scrapbooks were pretty primitive, but Dad and Mother appreciated each picture and Dad treasured each book as if it were an illuminated manuscript. This giving of oneself as well as the giving of a tangible gift is most precious, both to the giver and the recipient.

The Long Island Agronomist

The English language was Dad's instrument, as the violin was Kreisler's or the piano Paderewski's, but *only* when he was speaking. As a speaker, he was a real spellbinder. He might wander from the track but he'd get back, and he never lost an audience. But when he got down to the written word he got all tied up in his sentences. His rambling syntax and intricate embellishments could get completely out of hand. This was not handwritten stuff either. He dictated, and taking down Dad's dictation was a job for a saint. I took it more than once and to sit and sit while he evolved one of his elaborate and convoluted sentences was not easy.

Dad's unique writing style reached full flowering in the *Long Island Agronomist*, that small monthly publication that he wrote and Mother edited. In the Farewell Number he describes both its beginnings and its end. After telling the story of the development of the two experimental farms, he continues:

> The so-called "phenomenal success" of both [farms] No.1 and No. 2 created wide-spread interest and brought from far and wide requests for detailed information. Mr. Peters then authorized the publication of a semi-monthly circular, the first number being published August 1st, 1907. This twice-a-month proposition was found to be difficult to handle, for those in charge of the work were not trained writers and the vast amount of detail arising from the planting and caring for upwards of 1,000 different varieties made a less frequent issue a necessity and the *Long Island Agronomist* became a monthly, appearing without a single break on the first day of each month.
>
> The subscription list used for the first issue numbered about 600 persons. This list grew...until requests to the number of 16,000 had reached the *Long Island Agronomist* office and the little publication...was sent to every part of the world, not only to the well-recognized civilized portions of the globe, but to many still deemed at least semi-barbarous.

His farewell is typically long-winded:

> This number of the *Long Island Agronomist* carries to its every reader a heartfelt good-bye, so long, farewell, *adios, auf wiedersehen, gluck auf, adieu*, and *hasta luego*. Those responsible for the words placed before you in its many issues since August 1907 regret that their limited educations prevent them from using all the heartfelt phrases of farewell used by its readers in whose veins flows the blood of Greece, Russia, Italy, Denmark, Sweden, Portugal, Japan, China, South Africa, India, Haiti, Philippine Islands, Korea, Scotland, Ireland, Wales, Hungary, Poland, Austria, or Turkey. On another page the whys and wherefores of this polyglot farewell are set forth.

So to another page:

> ...because of the financial stringency felt by all railroads in the Eastern states, Long Island's transportation company has had to make radical reductions in each and every one of its departments.
>
> The *Agronomist* is therefore suspended for an indefinite period and those responsible for its articles hope in all sincerity that remembrances of it may be kindly ones, and that its readers, past and present, realize fully that its sole endeavor has been to help in every way, manner, and form all those with a yearning for life in the open, as well as placing in its proper position the now far famed Blessed Island.

Between 1907 and 1910 the *Agronomist* was issued at Huntington. There should be a plaque on the little red barn that still stands behind our house on Main Street but who would know what it was all about? Time certainly marches on and leaves much in the dust by the roadside.

When all operations moved to Medford in 1910, perforce the *Agronomist* went along, but it was still printed in Huntington by the Suffolk Bulletin printing shop. At first the Medford office was in one of the ubiquitous boxcars but eventually another portable house was put up just south of the road that bisected the farm. There were two rooms full of typists and files and things, and Dad and Mother each had a small office.

Hartie was Chief Clerk and general manager of the office and it became a veritable hive of industry. I don't know how many clerks were on hand at any given time but they must have come and gone, for I remember a lot of them. The volume of mail and Dad's long-winded answers to "each and every one" certainly made for an awful lot of work for the office force. Then there were all kinds of compilations of the results of his experiments, and the monthly summaries of weather information.

Another chore for the office staff was tending the weather stations. At Wading River Dad had set up a recording thermometer and hygrometer to accurately record his fabulous weather. He set up another station at Medford and

HBF tending the weather station at Medford, c.1914

eventually he had them all over the Island. Some were in the charge of other weather buffs but some had to be serviced from the Farm once a week. So somebody from the office made the rounds—by train—and that certainly shot a day. At Medford Dad also had a rain gauge and an anemometer. Tending the weather station there was one of his favorite chores.

Going back to Dad's writing style, he writes of the dairy:

> Absolute cleanliness was not only next to godliness but it was a prime necessity as well, and [was] the most important item in the handling of the lacteal fluid, whether for sale as such, or in golden bricks to aid human beings' internal economy in disposing of the "staff of life."

This came under the heading of "Mineola Fair Memories":

> We are honored by the friendship of many of the most fervent upholders of woman's right to vote. We listened with interest and with hearty approval to logical...appeals in clear-cut English...yet saw and heard marked proof that many a vote would be lost to the cause these undoubtedly earnest women were espousing, because most strikingly was displayed that invention said to have emanated from the disordered brain of some Parisian man-dressmaker, which has for its existence in a woman's skirt no reason based on utility, grace, beauty or modesty, and to this was added another item, undoubtedly conceived with the idea of drawing attention to the cause for which the speakers were making

such earnest pleas, and which unquestionably accomplished this object, while at the same time losing many a certain vote, for the considerable assembly of men and women who saw this invasion of the walks in Floral Hall by a saddle horse, without exception showed by looks, by action and even by most forceful phrases that their disapproval was practically unanimous.

Now, as nearly as I can interpret this, there was a demonstration for women's suffrage at the fair, and apparently the women involved were wearing that fashionable fad, the hobble skirt, with the slit up the side, and somebody must have ridden through Floral Hall on horseback. There were times when clarity was definitely missing in Dad's writing.

He had the greatest collection of little phrases and catchwords that he used over and over. Some were reflections of his early days or the earlier days he remembered hearing about. One of his favorites was, "The latchstring is always out." This appeared at the end of each of the later issues of the *Agronomist* and in many a letter. I have a feeling it calls for an explanation in this day of Yale locks and keys. In the days when you built your own house of logs or lumber worked from trees of your own felling, you also made your own door and door latch which was a simple catch on the inside operated from the outside by a string that hung through a hole. To lock up at night you merely pulled in the latchstring. When feeling hospitable, you left the latchstring out.

"Light and tie" was a cordial greeting, and when anyone left they "hit the pike." "Calamity howlers" were the dismal people who felt that the world was "going to the everlasting bow-wows." To them he would "give the merry ha-ha" for he was the eternal optimist. He used poker terms like "ante up," "stand pat," "hands down." He taught us to play poker and we had many a game in the long winter evenings. We had no idea it was a gambler's game and the cause of many a shooting in the wild and wooly west.

Things were "top notch," it was a "cast iron cinch," a book was "chock-full" of good information. As a railroad man, he referred to other men as either "broad gauge" or "narrow gauge." He also had another term that eludes me. He refers to "high-hook farmers." Any relation to "top notch?"

He was forever "proving conclusively" that "each and every one" of his projects was "a howling success." But the really overworked word was "neighbor." Very handy if you hadn't the faintest idea who the man was that you were greeting so effusively. "Howdy, Neighbor" served fine. The *Agronomist* is full of such remarks as, "Neighbor Lupton of Mattituck stopped by," and he refers to "Neighbor Lippincott of the Pennsylvania Railroad." He really stretched the word to the limit but it meant more to him than the fellow who lived next door. Every man was his neighbor because he used the term with all its connotations of mutual endeavor. He would cooperate with anyone and expected them to cooperate with him.

There were two words he lived by: Loyalty and Patriotism. Patriotism was next to godliness in his eyes and the American flag flew at both farms from the days of their inception to the end of the era. He also believed in the Brotherhood of Man and he combined his fierce devotion to the USA with his belief that all men are created free and equal and that among the hordes of immigrants who were seeking a decent life over here at that time there was brain and ambition and industry as well as mere muscle. In the *Agronomist* he expresses his thoughts on this subject at great length.

As for the wonders which Long Island had wrought:

> Long Island has done a heap for the world....It was the site of the first custom house, academy and lighthouse. It furnished the food for man and beast that enabled the little hamlets of New York City and Brooklyn to develop, after making of itself a barrier to the ocean's buffetings, forming thereby the magnificent harbor which built up for the Empire State the biggest city in the world. It furnished two governors and the most famous of the country's presidents [Teddy Roosevelt]. The finest oysters, asparagus, clams, ducks, fruits and plant seeds....It produced both the men who announced that they had discovered the North Pole [Cook and Peary]....Neighbor Goethals who connected the Atlantic and Pacific Oceans via Panama. No part of the United States has produced a continuous performance of good things for close on to three centuries, except the Blessed Isle.

In browsing through the *Agronomist*, I am fascinated to meet many old friends—variety names I had forgotten long ago. On a farm like ours you didn't just have potatoes or strawberries for supper, you had Gold Coin or Quick Lunch potatoes and William Belt or Chesapeake strawberries. Most likely you had both, and discussed their relative merits.

Some of the names are rather charming. Kleckly Sweet and Halbert Honey watermelons, Black Red Ball beet, Howling Mob sweet corn, French Breakfast and White Icicle radishes, not to mention the Sakurajima radish. This was a great big Japanese radish that achieved thirty pounds in its native Japan. Dad got it up to thirteen pounds. It was crisp and white and when it was peeled and sliced thin it was as good as any tiny radish. It could even be stored and used through the early part of the winter.

As for cantaloupes—ah, the sweet memories! There was Emerald Gem and Netted Gem, Rocky Ford and Jenny Lind, to mention just a few. They must have had Dad's full attention one year for I can well remember the huge piles of them at the end of their rows, ours for the eating. That was one great thing about living on an experimental farm. The produce was not raised for market—except for the Home Hampers—and we at the Farm were the ultimate consumers. Much went to feed the stock because we couldn't eat it all. But we kids did our best on that muskmelon patch. We took ourselves and a carving knife down to the field. I can even tell you where it was—just south of the cow barn. And we sat ourselves down very much like the Walrus and the Carpenter and we worked our way through the melons just as they took on the oysters. We would cut a melon and tentatively taste it. If it was good, we ate it; if not of exquisite flavor and texture and aroma we impatiently tossed it aside and tried another one. With each one we got more and more critical. This was a fine way to weed out the poorer varieties. An untouched pile meant they weren't worth our time; a heap of scooped-out shells meant A-OK.

We knew all the varieties of everything on the place and ate accordingly. Grape season was a beautiful time. There was a good-sized vineyard by the office and half of the path to the track was planted with grape vines trained on bamboo arches. The little piles of grape skins marked our progress. We left the Delawares pretty much alone for Mother loved them and they were saved for her. They were dainty, sweet little red beads of juice and flavor. Dad liked the big white Niagara. I did a great deal of sampling from the Niagara to the Concord to the Worden (a super Concord) but always ended up at the Agawam vine on the path. This was a red one, rather coarse in texture but of a sweet spiciness that made me purr like a kitten.

Of the plums, the Satsuma was my favorite. I think we only had Japanese plums—four varieties—although there may have been German prunes too. These plums were wonderfully prolific and hung as thick as swarms of bees on the branches. There was the Wickson, whose Japanese name was Ekuri, the Burbank (or Smomo), Abundance (or Botan), and my dear Satsumas.

Mother liked the Ekuri. It was a beautiful plum, a rose-gold heart-shaped fruit, but it was too sweet and juicy for me, and was a clingstone which made it messy to eat. The Satsuma was the darkest red that red can be, with a hazy bloom. The flesh was a dark red color clear through and it came away from the pit clean so you could pull it apart like a freestone peach. My pockets bulged with these plums from the first to ripen to the last.

We even had our favorite vegetable varieties. A sweet young Chantenay carrot made a pleasant change from peaches or plums or melons. Thomas Laxton peas were great too, and you could fill your pockets with the big pods, find a comfortable spot and pop your way through them.

Those Gold Coin potatoes I remember as being small, round, russet potatoes that baked to an ineffable fluffiness. Dad does not speak kindly of them in the early days but mentions them as being good in a later copy of the *Agronomist*. Perhaps they did better when the farm had been worked for some years. I was delighted to meet the Gold Coin potato again in Gladys Hasty Carroll's book, *As the Earth Turns*. Dad always stole enough little new potatoes from a few hills so we could have the first new potatoes along with peas and strawberry shortcake on Hope's birthday, June 10.

Among Dad's many projects were sugar beets. He first grew them in 1912, and in the *Agronomist* he discussed the question of sugar production at great length. They did grow well, ranked high in sugar content, and it seemed like the dawning of a new industry for Long Island. For years the prospect of a sugar beet factory on the Island was discussed and it very nearly came to pass. The Polish farmers in the Riverhead area were much interested. I don't know why it fell through. Dad was madly testing with seed from France, Austria, Germany, and anywhere else they were raised.

In 1922, I went to Denver with Dad and Mother to a meeting of the Railway Development Association, a national organization of the agricultural departments of most of the country's railroads. We went to visit a sugar beet factory while we were there, and there was much talk about the industry for Long Island so I know he was still waging the good fight at that time. At what point the whole thing petered out I don't know. Anyway, this shows Dad's persistence when he was after something for Long Island—ten years on sugar beets. They at least made excellent cattle food so it was no waste.

For several years Dad battled for a State Agricultural School for Long Island. This was first proposed in 1909 but the bill to create the school was not passed until 1912. A Board of Directors was appointed at this time. Among the men on the board was Ezra A. Tuttle, who often appears in the *Agronomist* and who eventually became Hope's father-in-law.

Dad immediately composed a "school yell" which he seemed to consider as important as the charter:

L.I.A.U! L.I.A.U!
INSECTICIDE AND FUNGICIDE AND FERTILIZER TOO!
L. I. AG. UNIVERSITY!
RAH! RAH! RAH!

By 1914, a staff was forming and the school was shaping up at Farmingdale. Dad always figured women should have an equal opportunity with men and I think he had a lot to do with the inclusion of girls at Farmingdale. I think Hope went there in the fall of 1917 so she was a member of one of their first classes. After two years she graduated as a finished poultry aficionado.

Getting an agricultural education up to this time had not been easy for Long Islanders. Cornell had summer courses—six weeks, if a farm lad could spare the time and cash to go to Ithaca. There were Extension Schools held on the Island during the winter, with short courses in various phases of farming. The idea that farming could be considered a science was catching on, and the "good enough for Grandpa" men were beginning to realize that anyone can learn and that sometimes new ways are better ways. Also, the young people were reaching out and fathers were realizing that it was smart to let them go get some "book learning" and bring it back to the family operation.

The LIRR organized Boys' Clubs in 1912 for boys under twenty-one and offered prizes for excellence in the raising of potatoes and corn, the three standard crops. This was followed in 1914 by Long Island Homemakers' Clubs for girls. These clubs for young people anticipated the 4-H Clubs that are a vital part of the life of farm young people even in these days.

Dad waged many other battles. One was for pure seed—acceptance of responsibility by the seller for providing clean seed and not a mixture of crop and weed seed. He accepted the need for testing cows for tuberculosis when it was first realized that milk was a source of infection. In these days, tuberculosis is not considered one of life's major hazards, but in the early days of the century it was the big killer. Living conditions had much to do with it. Before it was learned that the biggest source of contagion was contaminated milk, many a woman or child just faded away from "consumption."

When the idea of testing cows came up, and the further idea of condemning cows that were infected with tuberculosis, there was an uproar from cow owners. But the cows at the Farm were all tested early in the game and one of our best ones went, as well as a young bull that was Dad's pride. Dad went along with them to the slaughterhouse with his camera and I'm sure his pictures of infected lungs, printed in the *Agronomist*, helped in the crusade.

In his announcement that as of January, 1910 the *Agronomist* would be sent to its readers (at that time there were 10,000 of them) on a monthly rather than bimonthly basis, he says:

> ...the *Agronomist* will be issued on the first day of each month and will never be dated a month or so ahead in accordance with the weird custom so prevalent today with those who publish huge magazines, full of pages, some of which are partly filled with other matter besides the illustrations and striking margins.

When a letter to the editor suggested that "a more severe, dignified style should be adopted" Dad replied:

> We have never felt that the *Agronomist*'s mission was to illustrate the highest ideals of literary possibilities or monumental typographical excellence, or that it was so invaluable that even its margins should be preserved for future earth dwellers. The best we can do is to put in fairly readable shape, with the assistance of our able co-workers in field, in office and in editorial den, the open-air happenings we encounter in our heart-felt efforts to discover ways and means to aid and develop the Blessed Isle.

After seven years, the *Agronomist* ceased publication in November of 1914.

Necromantic Wizardism

Dad waged a running battle with all the plant wizards and nature fakers. The early part of the century was a time of wide-eyed innocence as far as the general public was concerned and the theory of evolution was looked at askance by the rank and file. "As it was in the beginning, is now and ever shall be, world without end" applied to that supreme achievement of the Lord's—mankind—and all the living things of man's world.

On the other hand, any freak of nature was of intense interest. The two-headed calf, the bearded lady, the giant and the midget were the stock in trade of the circus sideshow. They were gazed upon avidly but in fear and trembling. The Cardiff Giant—that magnificent hoax—really shook the country. Anything other than the normal that violated the sweet, peaceful progress of the world and mankind through the ages was suspect.

The curiosity about the freaks in the sideshow carried over into curiosities in the plant world and there were those who took good advantage of man's credulity. As P.T. Barnum said, "There's a sucker born every minute." A splendid example of this came to Dad's attention in 1910. Let him tell it:

> Last year we read a pathetic story about a man who, having raised an orange tree from his only daughter's bridal wreath, longed to have some sentimental reminder before him all summer, so he crossed the blossoms of this orange tree with his favorite cucumber, the result, according to the story, being a beautiful orange-shaped fruit nestling midst the dark green leaves of the cucumber beetle's favorite plant. The flesh was described as the most delicious blending of the finest Florida orange with the crispness of the unassuming cucumber. This sentimental child of nature offered (because of his love for his daughter) to sell seeds of this cucumber for one dollar apiece, and only one to

a person. We didn't buy any of these seeds, although very sentimental ourselves, because we knew the orange cucumber under its earlier name of lemon cucumber, and we further knew that it was of no value except as an additional attraction for exhibition purposes.

Unfortunately, the sophisticated folk of today are just as easily taken in by the nature fakers, and the nurseries that sell climbing strawberries and instant shade trees are doing just as well as did the gentleman with his orange blossom cucumber.

In the *Agronomist* again, Dad takes issue with what he calls "Necromantic Wizardism."

> Undoubtedly a vast number of things that never happened have been reported by agricultural song-and-dance men and acrobatic back-to-nature boomers.
>
> Charity leads us to think that at times the marvelous impossibilities are discovered by those who are just learning that potatoes grow underground and corn pretty well up in the air. Common sense at other times causes us to recognize the footprints of the merry press agent, earning his stipulated salary or his uncertain commission by puncturing his gas bag for revenue alone.

This kind of thing would take Dad veritable hours to compose. He would smoke the inevitable cigarette, gaze out the window and grope for the tasty phrase like that Necromantic Wizardism. At times like this, any secretary who had struggled to learn shorthand wondered why she ever bothered. You could not only follow him in longhand, you could have done it in Egyptian hieroglyphics. To continue:

> We recently read a report of a lecture given under the auspices of an institution established on popular educational lines that showed there were still openings for not only the improbable but the utterly impossible as well. A report appearing in a conservative, high-class publication credited various weird statements to the gentleman who uses sections of the alphabet as a tail to his name. For instance, in crediting occult creations to one occupying considerable printers' ink in the agricultural world, the lecturer stated that said printers' "inkarion" is so deeply grounded in the natural sciences that he does not try crossing utterly different species, but takes things of the same family, combining strawberries, raspberries, blackberries and the apple. We are not way up even on Gray's Botany, but we feel that any attempt to have strawberries borne on apple trees or apples borne on vines will end up in a disastrous Waterloo. We feel very certain that even Providence (now so seldom credited with plant life achievements) could not be convinced that such a change would be an advance, even from man's point of view.

This "inkarion" must have been Luther Burbank. As I remember it, Luther Burbank was to be classed with that evil man, the Commission Merchant. Dad had no good word to say for him. According to Dad, Burbank was making wild claims of "creating" new and marvelous plants practically out of thin air. Dad claimed that Burbank's spineless cactus, which was supposed to prove a boon to the cattle raisers in arid countries, was found in Mexico, moved to California, and introduced as the Plant Wizard's own creation. The Burbank plum was nothing more nor less than the Smomo plum of Japan, imported and renamed, and so on and so forth.

I knew my Dad too well to take everything he said at face value and I felt that Mr. B. should have his chance on the witness stand so I went to the library and looked up a book on Luther Burbank. There was only one book on the shelves and this was written by one Henry Smith Williams, the Secretary of the Luther Burbank Society and obviously an acolyte. The general tone of the book is what you would expect of a book written about St. Peter by the Third Assistant Gatekeeper. The Great Man is so great that we tiptoe through the pages. He was a super genius of the plant world.

As nearly as I can determine, Burbank was without any technical or scientific training, but he had a keen interest in plants and a very observant eye for all the differences in individuals. With no knowledge of Mendel or his laws of heredity, Burbank embarked on his mission of improving or changing strains by hybridization and selection, generation after generation.

He got a flying start with his first "creation." While working on his father's farm, he found a seed pod on a potato plant. Out of curiosity he planted the seed and hit the jackpot. One seed yielded a potato that was such a vast improvement over the current varieties that it became *the* potato, was named the Burbank, and netted him enough to take him from the Massachusetts farm to California. He made enough money in the nursery business to set himself up as an experimenter. So it would seem he was also a very smart businessman. Once the publicity about plant wizardry (or Necromantic Wizardism) was started, it gained momentum very quickly and he was able to sit back and modestly accept the plaudits.

The Third Assistant Gatekeeper viewed him, with bated breath, as a genius capable of anything. Dad viewed him as a charlatan and refused to admit that any man can "create" any form of plant life. He might have accepted a claim of "developing" a new variety, but the word "create" stuck in his craw.

Let's face it. Dad had no scientific background either, and he became an "agricultural expert." He learned by reading and by experience. But he only claimed to raise great cabbages and melons—he didn't claim he created them. Burbank, in his field of "plant creation," came up with a lot of things that were more interesting than useful. His white blackberry never set the world on fire; his stoneless plums certainly are not now on the market; there are no great plantings of his spineless cactus. He spent twenty-five years trying to cross two nightshades and finally got one pod of seed. From this he came up with the Sunberry. What this is or was I do not know, but you won't see it in the produce market today or find it listed in any nursery catalog. I will have to admit that I was so brainwashed in my youth that I can't consider Burbank with the awe the world accorded him, but certainly the book I got hold of did nothing to change my mind.

These two men—Dad and Mr. B.—clashed violently over a melon. In a 1910 *Agronomist* article summarizing the year's results with various crop varieties, we find the following:

> The much lauded Burbank cantaloupe creation turned out to be a fuzzy, slim, elongated curiosity, rather pointed at the blossom end, flat and insipid in flavor, somewhat like a cross between a raw citron and a squash.

This was in the November 1 edition. On November 9, the following letter was written at Santa Rosa, California:

Dear Sir,

In your monthly record of so-called "facts" we notice you speak of a "much lauded Burbank cantaloupe creation."

We ask you with exceeding great respect, who lauded it? Who sent it to you? Whose creation is it? Whose "elongated curiosity" was it, this cross between a raw citron and a squash?

Mr. Burbank never sent out a cantaloupe creation in his life. That's all.

Respectfully,

Luther Burbank
per P.W.O. Sec.

To which Dad responded on November 17:

Dear Sir,

Herewith is tendered an acknowledgement of your letter dated November 9th, 1910.

It is scarcely necessary to say that its contents are surprising indeed.

Your first paragraph, we feel, should not have been written until the questions which appear in your second paragraph had been answered (if at all).

Your third paragraph we most cordially welcome, for we are in accord with the many educated mortals in feeling very certain that some power far greater than any known to humankind is alone responsible for all creations.

Regarding your second paragraph, to categorically name the many who lauded would, we acknowledge with regret, require time and space which would, we feel certain, encroach as heavily upon your crowded moments as upon our own, for many, many publications have a place in the extremely long list.

Your two questions, "Whose creation was it?" and "Whose elongated curiosity was it?" are of course but the same question changed only by a phrase more fitting and proper than the word creation, which of course cannot be properly applied to either selections, crosses, or hybrids, even though they be partially due to the efforts of humankind.

The seed was not sent but given to us by one whose uprightness and veracity long ago placed him in an enviable position.

We will make an earnest endeavor to secure names, dates and addresses in time for Volume 4, Number 5 of the *Long Island Agronomist*, which will be issued as usual on the first of the month. Had we supposed that such data would have been of interest to any of our 12,000 readers, we should have tried to secure it in time for the issue of November 1st, in which we mentioned the fact, which, as it was an actual happening during the growing season of 1910, could not, we contend, be properly designated as a "so-called" fact, because in verity it was and is, and hence always must be, an exact and well-authenticated fact; therefore, to summarize, we are justified before all men in taking exception to your first paragraph, recognizing the pertinency of your second paragraph, and receiving with heartfelt gratitude your assurance regarding at least one of the many "creations" which we have seen credited to Neighbor Burbank of California.

We sincerely trust that this same disclaimer covers as well, many of the other foods for man and beast which were long ago placed upon the earth by a power, natural or supernatural, far beyond the most supreme effort of any mortal.

Very truly yours,

The Long Island Agronomist
by Hal B. Fullerton,
Compiler

N.B. — Just in time to catch this number of the *Agronomist*, we find the following data given us by the donor of the above mentioned cantaloupe seed, and quote verbatim: "I purchased from Mr. Luther Burbank a lot of new creations that have cost several thousand dollars, and I have secured a new melon that is a wonder." Much detail regarding size, etc. follows, but lack of space prevents the printing.

Mr. Burbank's henchman lost no time in answering this, and on November 23 wrote:

Dear Sir,

Your long and highly interesting letter of November 17th received.

We would recommend you to look into Webster's, Worcester's or the International Dictionary and study what is said under word "creation." Perhaps you never looked this matter up. We have recently received a number of orders for the melon from your advertisement, several from Long Island, the parties stating that they judged that you did not know how to raise melons. We are doing very well, thank you.

Heartily thanking you for your advertisement, we are,

Respectfully yours,

Luther Burbank
per P.W.O. Sec.

To this, Dad replied on December 7:

Glad to receive your favor of the 23rd.

Your recommendation was received in the kindly spirit in which it was undoubtedly sent. I beg to assure you, however, that the definition of the word "creation" has been known to us for many years.

Pleased to know that the *Long Island Agronomist* is still living up to the principle upon which it was started, that is, that in its humble way it might prove helpful to others.

I should judge that our Long Island neighbors who you say have written you ordering melons, and stating that they judged that we did not know how to raise melons, have never tasted the many fine melons of various varieties Long Island's benign climate and particularly good soil have produced upon the Long Island R.R. Experimental Stations of which we are in charge.

We most fervently pray that these Long Islanders who are contemplating giving up part of their melon patches to this variety which proved so valueless to us, will secure melons of sufficient merit to cover all items of expenditure.

We note that you are again in error, as we print no advertisements whatsoever; we simply note those things which prove of value, as well as those which clearly demonstrate the fact that they are unsuited to Long Island conditions, or are lacking in merit as human food.

Most sincerely yours,

H.B. Fullerton,
Dir. Agricultural
Development

Bamboo grown at Medford made this graceful archway that was later covered with grape vines.

These two letters he captions, "Final 'Creation' Documents."

I can't say who came out on top of this strange altercation. One can hardly call it an argument. It seems more like two small boys sticking their tongues out at each other.

A man of a very different type was David Fairchild, the head of the Bureau of Plant Introduction, a branch of the U.S. Department of Agriculture. He and Dad got to be good friends.

Mr. Fairchild wrote a fascinating book covering his years with plant introductions called *The World Is My Garden*, and in it I met many of the plants that we tried out on the Farm. The purpose of the Bureau was to find new and useful plants for one or another segment of the American agricultural world. This meant trying out these new plants under varying conditions as they came into the country. The LIRR Demonstration Farm became one of his testing grounds, to Dad's great delight. It added to the census of plants grown on the Farm and when something grew successfully it was another feather in the bonnet of the Blessed Isle.

This was the era of the plant explorer and men were off in all corners of the world collecting plants. The Bureau's "Chinese Wilson" was bringing in fabulous lilies from such strange places as Nepal and Tibet, and the Arnold Arboretum was becoming a treasure house of rare plants, but these were not "creations"—they were acquisitions. They were certainly used in hybridizing and developing new types, but the three-ring circus aura of Burbank's work was entirely missing.

The bamboo that still grows at Medford, beside the garage at St. James, and on the farm at Middle Island, came originally from David Fairchild and the Bureau of Plant Introduction. This has always been a great curiosity and one of Dad's favorite talking points—Long Island is able to grow bamboo! It came from northern China so is perfectly hardy. It may not grow large enough to use for building houses or shoring up roadside ditches (as we later saw bamboo used in Trinidad) but it makes great plant stakes and fishing poles and conversation pieces. It can also become a menace. It spreads just like quackgrass and it took over the entire area at Medford from the pump house to the road. This, however, was long after Dad left the Farm.

Udo was imported from Japan and also grew with wild abandon, seeding itself in unlikely places. This was originally grown like asparagus and was hilled up in the spring to blanch the shoots. It had a faint flavor of turpentine and was not really popular with any of us but Dad. He enthused over anything that he grew. He says in the *Agronomist*:

> Without reservation of any description we now positively pronounce this Japanese salad plant a decided acquisition to the American table. It favors both celery and asparagus but is very different from either....

Then we had dasheen. This came from somewhere in the tropics but accepted the not-quite-tropic climate that Dad offered. Dad says that "its tuber, when cooked, reminds one instantly of boiled chestnuts, and with nearly everyone quickly finds favor." I'm sorry, but as I remember it, it cooked down to a grayish mush and was not all that sought after.

In one shipment from Washington there was a tea plant. All these tender things were planted south of the pump house where they had a sunny southern exposure and protection from the north winds of winter. The tea was planted here along with whatever other exotics came along with it. The next spring the tea plant had survived sufficiently to put forth two leaves. With this it gave up the ghost but the word went out on the strength of the two leaves: "Tea grows on Long Island." We never got as far as coffee.

French artichokes grew around the place and seeded themselves happily. They made handsome, prickly plants with beautiful big thistle flowers. I don't think we ate them. I have a feeling nobody knew *how* to eat an artichoke, but they were very ornamental and most attractive to the bumblebees.

The Japanese walnuts that grew around the place and the Japanese poplar that was such a fine, fast-growing shade tree came from Washington. The latter was very successful until it reached blooming age. Then the fuzzy cotton that flew with the seeds became a real nuisance. There was one between the house and horse barn and it succeeded in clogging up the window screens of the kitchen to the point where they let in neither light nor air.

Dad and Mother met with David Fairchild on their trips to Washington but I don't think he ever came to the Farm. His name, however, was a household word.

Sea Pines, a School of Personality

In the spring of 1914 we went to New York and met the Reverend Thomas Bickford who was owner and Director of Sea Pines School for Girls at Brewster on Cape Cod. I believe we met him in the waiting room at Grand Central Station so he must have been on his way back to school. He apparently decided that we were acceptable types for he agreed that Hope should enter after the Easter vacation and I should follow in the fall.

I don't know what precipitated this going off to boarding school. Perhaps Dad and Mother had planned it this way all along. Perhaps they had come to realize that we were living too isolated a life and that we should go where we could mingle with our own kind.

In September we were both packed up and went off to Cape Cod. Mother went along to see us settled. I was twelve at the time and went into the eighth grade. I can't recall much of the first days there but I don't recall being unduly homesick or confused. I liked school. I liked study, and I had no trouble.

The Rev. Mr. Bickford was known as Father Bickford, his wife Mother Bickford (although they were really more grandfatherly and grandmotherly in age) and their two daughters were Miss Faith and Miss Addie. He was a dandy person and a fine man to have a hand in the evolvement of the personalities of young girls. He looked a good deal like Mr. Pickwick. He had a great sense of humor and a real love of humankind, and his feet were solidly on the ground. His blue eyes twinkled but also looked straight through you. He had been a Presbyterian minister, but it was not a Presbyterian school by any means.

We had a short evening service after supper. On Sunday this was sometimes a Glee Club concert, or it was in the charge of one special group or another. At Thanksgiving, Christmas, and Easter, we had story readings. Stories written in

English classes had been turned in for judgement. It was overwhelmingly exciting when Miss Faith would arise and announce that the story she was about to read had been written by Eleanor Fullerton. I did pretty well in this department. They were all stories about girls "finding themselves" and could be pretty sentimental. But it was a sentimental age, I'm afraid, and Sea Pines fostered the emotional approach.

In those days, one was expected to conform to the ideals set by one's elders. For us this was no struggle—we never thought of any other way of life than that led by our parents and grandparents. Changes in thinking came so slowly that they were hardly noticed. The big upheavals in attitudes were far in the future.

The schoolroom was but a part of Sea Pines. It was a School of Personality and its major purpose was the pursuit of the Good, the True, and the Beautiful. There was a system of awards for what was called personality development. The first award was the winning of the Red.

We wore a school uniform—blue serge middy and great baggy bloomers, long black or white stockings, and shoes of our choice, usually white sneakers. A black or white necktie was tied in a sailor's knot and worn until you won the Red and then—and only then—could you wear a red necktie. Winning the Red indicated that a girl was on the right track. It had to be won every year.

Red Sunday came once a month. Everyone wore a white Norfolk jacket outfit, which might be called our dress uniform, and the first Sunday of the year it was a sea of white. After that, those who were entitled to wear the red tie did so. There was a heap of little red ribbons on the podium and a lovely pile of red roses. Miss Faith read the name of each girl in turn, and each went up and received her bit of red ribbon, a red rose, and a slip of paper with an uplifting verse which was thenceforth hers alone. I still have the bit of red ribbon that was pinned to my blouse in October of 1917 and the verse that went with it: "All things are possible to him who believes."

The second award was the red armband of the Awakener. What they really meant by an Awakener I don't know. I *think* they meant one who was a good kid and would be a good influence on others. I won the Awakener's red armband in November of 1915, and in 1916 the white armband of the Junior Counsellor.

Junior Counsellors were considered leaders and very responsible citizens. Among other privileges, they could go off the grounds at will. With the school's many acres, this was hardly necessary, but one did want to walk the two miles to the store and back now and then, and the company of a Junior Counsellor was necessary. She went along as surety for good behavior, I suppose.

The Junior Counsellors also had the responsible job of turning off the lights. Turn off the lights? A mere babe in arms can flip a switch and turn off a light! Ah, so you can, if you have electricity, but we had gas lights. There was one gas jet per room plus the many in main rooms, corridors and classrooms. This eliminated the coziness of desk lamps and floor lamps but served our purposes well enough.

Eleanor in her Sea Pines School uniform, 1919

I think the reason that I was not homesick at Sea Pines was that I was in familiar country. Cape Cod and Long Island have much in common ecologically speaking. The pitch pines grew from the back of the tennis courts clear down to the dunes along Cape Cod Bay. The same bayberry and sweet fern, wild roses, goldenrod and asters grew in the open places. Beach grass and sand dunes were not unfamiliar to me. The cranberry bogs were like the ones out in Calverton, and bearberry (which they called kinnikinnick on the Cape) covered sandy areas. I loved their exquisite pink bells in the spring, as I loved the minute white violets that grew in the sphagnum moss on the edges of the bogs.

An open spot in the pine woods was the setting for the Commencement play each June and I loved nothing more than dramatics. I'm sure I wasn't a good actress but I nearly always came through the tryouts with a part of some sort. My first year, the play was *As You Like It*, and I was tapped to play Touchstone, the fool.

The costumes were rented from French's in Boston but Mother and Dad felt they could concoct a fool's costume and they certainly did. They went to New York to the Metropolitan to do their research. Then Dad designed the whole thing, between them they figured out how to make it, and Mother took over with her seamstress skills.

It was a howling success. It was a red and yellow parti-colored outfit made of sateen. The jacket had points around the bottom with a bell on each one. There was one long red silk stocking and one long yellow stocking sewed to a cut-off pair of Dad's long underwear, covered by short pantaloons. The shoes with points up the heel and curled pointed toes were made of tailors' stiffening. Bells jingled on all these points too. The headgear with a properly tufted cockscomb fell around the neck and shoulders, again with belled points. They made a bauble using the head of Punch from a Punch and Judy set. Even if I had been a total loss as Touchstone, that costume would have lighted up the play. I tremble to think how many hours went into the making of it, but that is the kind of thing Dad and Mother did.

We gave some good plays in that theater, usually Shakespeare—*The Tempest, The Merchant of Venice* and, of course, *As You Like It*. One year we did *The Pied Piper*. I was a monk in this one and we had to learn a Latin chant to intone in procession, with hands in our brown sleeves and our brown cowls over our heads. My Senior year I really did myself proud and captured the star part in *Captain Brassbound's Conversion*, by George Bernard Shaw. I was chosen, I think, because I was thin enough to pass in men's clothes and I could drop my voice to a properly piratical tone. Dad took a picture of the cast and I am hard to recognize behind the beard.

I was a member of the Industrial Group. We considered ourselves a very select group and we even had our own songs. One of them rather well explains:

> We are the Industrial Group,
> Teedle, eedle, dee, dee, dee!
> We wash the dishes and serve the soup,
> Teedle, eedle, dee, dee, dee!
> We make the sandwiches each one,
> And do it all with lots of fun.
> We sing our songs when we get done,
> Teedle, eedle, dee, dee, dee!

And that's what we did—a good share of the housework. We were the ones who needed some financial help in getting through school so we worked a certain number of hours a week for a certain sum credited to the tuition bill.

The serving room off the dining room was the rallying point for Industrials and was off-limits to ordinary mortals. There was a certain flair with which you pushed open the swinging door and disappeared from the common view. I don't know how this came about—that the worker bees were looked up to by the drones. Maybe because we obviously had a lot of fun. Nobody felt inferior for having to work her way—quite the contrary.

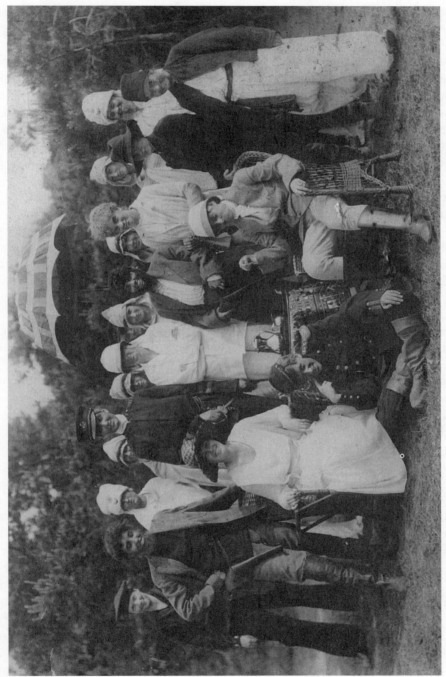

The cast of *Captain Brassbound's Conversion*. A bearded Eleanor, second from left, played the title role.

The waitresses were the queens of this group. I, for one, was terribly impressed when they swept through the swinging door one after the other, with huge trays held aloft, each bearing ten bowls of steaming soup. The graceful swoop with which each set her tray down on the stand I found most impressive.

I never achieved this status but I did have a pretty responsible job—that of delivering the mail. Hope had done it before me. Every girl had a correspondence list prepared by her parents, giving the names of those with whom she might correspond. My job was to sort the mail and check it with each girl's list and then slip the letters into the big envelopes that hung inside each door. The letters that had to pass the censor I took to Miss Addie's office and each recipient then had to identify her correspondent. Sometimes it was only Grandmother who had forgotten to put her name on the envelope, but it *might* be a brazen young man met during the last vacation who dared to address one of our young ladies. A request to have his name added to her list would have to go through parental channels.

I was also one of the early morning cleaners. We got up at 5:30 a.m. and went quietly to the serving room where crackers and mugs of milk awaited us and the brooms and dusters were hung in one corner. We cleaned classrooms, offices, living room and dining room every morning—without the aid of vacuum cleaners.

I also had the pleasure of ringing the rising bell. As it went "bong, bong, bong," I gleefully visualized all my dormant friends trying to ignore it, clutching pillows and hoping it was all a dream. A few more bongs for good measure and I would return to my broom and dustpan with the ridiculous self-satisfaction of the early riser contemplating the slugabeds.

The day was portioned off by that bell into classes, meals, rest hour when everyone was in her room reading or napping, recreation, which meant games or dancing or walking, study hall, room bell and, eventually, lights out. The young of today would be outraged at such a regimented life but I don't think it did us any harm to live within that orderly framework of the day. I liked it. I knew where I stood and where I was going next.

We made our own social life. Saturday night was party night. These parties were organized by different classes or by one of the various clubs. The junior class usually put on a pretty posh dance. But don't assume that this meant young gentlemen in their best, squiring our young ladies and leading them in a waltz, a two-step or the very modern one-step. There were no young gentlemen available and I doubt if they would have been allowed to enter our hallowed halls anyway.

I had one delightful term that was due to my mother's charm. She came up to the school once a month and talked on nature and gardens to the assembled school. She spent the night at the Homestead, the lovely old farmhouse where the Bickfords lived. I was invited to stay the night with her. I loved being with Mother and with Mother Bickford, and it was delightful to bed down under an old quilt in an old bed in an old room. And it was delightful to have a special breakfast with the ladies before I trotted back to school and classes.

An occasional outsider came to school for a talk or some kind of entertainment, and one I well remember was Katharine Lee Bates. She was an English professor at Wellesley and she read poetry for us—some of it her own—and interpreted it for us. At dinner at the head table afterward, she offered to exchange poems with anyone who was given to rhyme and rhythm. Three or four of us rushed off copies of what we considered our best. We timidly read them to Miss Bates, presented them to her, and retired bathed in a glow of shared poesy. In due time, we each received from her an autographed copy of "America the Beautiful." Some very astute soul set this to music and it is, to my mind, the perfect national anthem. The music is both beautiful and singable and the words are inspiring. My autographed copy is very precious to me.

There were occasional breaks in the routine of our lives. Thanksgiving vacation was a short one and Hope and I finally decided it was too much to take the long trip home. We discovered that it was actually tremendous fun to stay at school, even if it meant seeing boisterous friends off to their homes.

Much effort was put into making it enjoyable for the stay-at-schools. There was a grand and glorious Thanksgiving dinner, with the tables shoved around to make one long table, and we had all the good things that spell New England Thanksgiving. We even had pie for breakfast the day after, and that was certainly a real New England touch. As to that, we had baked beans every Saturday night, and ate the leftovers for Sunday morning breakfast. Fish chowder and fish hash were not ignored either.

May Day was a festive day and it involved a lot of folk dancing. It was held outdoors and we would worry about the weather. There was a May Queen and a Maypole. Never, under any circumstances, did the Maypole dance go right. We might start out with the grand right and left going neatly and the streamers weaving around the pole properly, but then some girl with two left feet would make a wrong move and throw everybody off so the pole ended up looking like a cat's cradle.

There was one holiday that was ours alone at Sea Pines and that was Arbutus Day. It always came as a complete surprise. One beautiful morning in early May, Miss Faith would announce at breakfast that this was Arbutus Day. It was a day of picnics and hikes and basking in the sun and reveling in Spring. Picnic lunches were packed and off we all went, by classes, to Blueberry Pond or to the beach or wherever, and came back late in the day, weary and sun-soaked. It was a grand day.

Dad and Mother always made much of our birthdays and when I was away at school they outdid themselves. The whole school must share it. One year they sent a great box of golden daffodils and I put one at each place at the supper tables. One year it was a box of little spice cupcakes. There was a candle for each one and when these were set around and the candles lighted it looked like a host of fireflies. I sat at the head table, and it was quite an occasion.

Hope graduated in 1917, wearing the graduation dress that Mother had made for her own graduation from Jenkintown Girls School back in the 1880s. At the reception that night, she wore a gorgeous creation in green and gold, her class colors. Once again, Dad designed it and Mother made it. As I remember, it was pale green taffeta with gold lace over it. It had puffed sleeves and a full skirt. They had a bouquet of gold roses and lilies-of-the-valley sent from Boston and she was as gorgeous as a Crown Princess.

When we came to my graduation in 1919, the whole picture had changed. During the War we had voted to forego elegant graduation finery in order to send that money for the care of a French war orphan. So, although the War was now ended, we wore the ubiquitous white Norfolk outfits for graduation and I wore the official family graduation dress that night, without flowers.

This was the first time I wore a long skirt and also the occasion upon which I put up my hair. In those prehistoric days, a girl wore short skirts and long hair up to a certain age, usually sixteen or seventeen, and then—bang!—she lowered her skirts and put her hair on top of her head and she was transformed from a child to a young lady.

It was a disappointment. It looked exactly the same from the front. The only change was the figure-eight bun at the back of my head instead of the two braids. But I was grown up. I was seventeen and I was graduated.

The folks came up for Commencement in the Model T and we all went back together. It was a two-day trip and we spent the night at Saunderstown, across from Newport, then puttered on the next day to catch the Bridgeport ferry. The roads were narrow and winding, the traffic practically nonexistent. We went through one quiet little town after another with miles of lovely open country between—a far cry from the New England Thruway.

World War I—The Home Front

In the summer of 1914, World War I broke out. I don't know why I remember it. Europe was light years away and there was always trouble in the Balkans. But I do remember the assassination at Sarajevo. It was just a newspaper item at the time.

But when Germany began her march through Belgium and France with her demand for *lebensraum*, the whole world sat up and took notice. France, England and Italy allied themselves to resist. Most Americans threw their sympathies with these Allies and many felt we should get into the fight immediately. But Woodrow Wilson was President and he was a most insistent Dove. He was a believer in isolationism and felt Europe's concerns were not ours.

There were many who did not agree with him and his slogan, "Too proud to fight." They were proud *to* fight and many a young man got there by way of the Canadian armed forces. Others—men and women both—went over to drive ambulances, or to man Red Cross canteens. The Lafayette Escadrille came into being, composed of young Americans who went over to fly the matchstick airplanes of 1914. After all, Lafayette had come to our assistance in 1776.

The evening of April 6, 1917, the Fullerton family went to the theater in New York. It must have been Easter vacation. I have no recollection of what we saw but I do remember coming out of the theater into a light spring rain and hearing the newsboys shouting, "Extra! Extra! Wilson declares war!"

Having stood on the sidelines for three years, the country threw itself into the war with wildest enthusiasm. Patriotism became the cardinal virtue and in many ways it exceeded the bounds of ordinary good sense. Anything and anybody German or with a taint of German became anathema.

People of German descent, or even with a German name, suffered. Many changed their names. My cousin May Pierce had married Harry Gestafeld and they changed their name to Guest. Anyone who owned a dachshund was looked upon as a German sympathizer, which was hard on both people and dachshunds. In a rather childish fashion, German iris became garden iris, sauerkraut became liberty cabbage, hamburgers liberty steaks, and frankfurters—was this when they became hot dogs?

Schools no longer taught German. I was sorely torn over this. I had been taking German for two years, had worked hard, and liked it. I had just started to read in German and was utterly charmed by the marvelous descriptive powers of the German compound words. *Im schwartzen trauerkleide* I felt expressed the depths of mourning much more sonorously than the mere words "in black clothes." However, I was an American and a Fullerton so I closed the German books, seized an American flag, and prepared to fight the war from Sea Pines.

I really did seize an American flag. We had a flagpole on the front lawn at Sea Pines and I was assigned the honorable job of lowering the flag every evening. Several of my friends might assist, stand at attention, and catch the stars and stripes so that they would not touch the ground. We even folded the flag in a military triangle and felt that the whole operation was very impressive.

Voluntary rationing came into being. Sugar, flour, meat, and fats became scarce so we were extra careful in our use of such commodities. Herbert Hoover was Food Administrator and I became the Herbert Hoover of Sea Pines. I went from girl to girl, and teacher to teacher, with a little pledge: "I will only use one spoonful of sugar on my cereal and one butter ball per meal" or some such. When an occasional girl refused to sign on the grounds that she "needed" sugar or butter, I was as outraged as if she had come out for the Kaiser.

At home we each had our week's allotment of sugar in a container at our place. It was up to us how we used it but what was left at the end of the week was pooled and if there was enough we had a dessert. Wheat flour was one of our scarcities and all the women taxed their ingenuity to come up with substitutes. Some of Mother's bread was more interesting than good as she struggled with soy meal and rice flour and her bread recipes.

A U-boat was sighted off the coast of Cape Cod which made the whole thing seem very close to us, and even Miss Faith's angelic temperament was ruffled by this daring. We bought Thrift Stamps with our allowance money, and some of us, by classes, adopted French war orphans. My class gave up graduation pomp, as I mentioned earlier, in favor of a French orphan.

We knitted, too. Everybody knitted, girls and teachers alike. Socks came off the needles in a steady stream. The unskilled could at least turn out a few yards of plain knitting and call it a scarf. Sweaters—khaki for the Army and blue for the Navy—took a little more skill. We made watch caps for the Navy and a sort of combination cap and face mask that was said to be a boon to the sailor standing watch on a destroyer. Wristlets were in demand. Unlike a glove or mitten, they did not cramp the trigger finger.

The Latin teacher, Miss Blanche, outdid us all. She was an Englishwoman and she knitted gray socks for the Tommies. She wore a gray dress and a man's gray sweater, her gray hair was screwed up in a bun at the back of her head, and steel-rimmed spectacles framed her cold gray eyes. She knitted straight through Latin class and the steel needles went "slish, slish" with the faintest pause as she shifted needles. She knitted as she breathed—automatically. And it was all rather mesmerizing, especially on test days. Then the Latin words and moods and tenses got all mixed up with the slishing from Miss Blanche's corner.

In the outside world, women carried their knitting wherever they went and no speaker or concert performer would dare suggest that the click and swish of needles and the occasional murmur of "knit two, purl two" was a mite disconcerting. I'd like to know how many garments my mother produced with her ever-busy needles.

At home, Dad was fighting the whole German army single-handedly. Flags sprouted everywhere on the Farm and the mantelpiece became a solid phalanx of framed photos of men in uniform. His favorite name for the German army was the "Pickelhaubes." This was the name of the German spiked helmet which must have been a direct descendent of the spiked helmets of the original Huns.

One of the first Army camps to be established was Camp Upton, where raw troops were brought in, equipped, given a minimum of training, and shipped overseas. Dad had a hand in the location of Camp Upton at Yaphank. The Army came to him and asked his advice on where to locate it. After all, who knew the Island better than Dad? I don't know why the decision was Yaphank, but that's where Camp Upton sprang up—a city of temporary buildings. Some of them were not so temporary, and are still in use at what is now Brookhaven National Laboratory.

One of the recruits was Irving Berlin and among his duties was the writing of the music for a Camp show. It was called "Yip, Yip, Yaphank," and the catchiest tune was "Oh, How I Hate to Get Up in the Morning." This show had a one-night stand at one of the New York theaters and we went in to see it. Irving Berlin himself sang the bugler song in his small voice, looking most ill-at-ease in his badly fitting uniform, campaign hat and wrap puttees. The final number was "Good-Bye Broadway, Hello France" and it was given the full treatment by the whole cast, marching with full pack off the stage, up the aisles, and out of the theater—ostensibly straight to the troop ships. Our patriotism fairly strangled us.

Once the military found Dad, they kept in touch with him and in the course of time the Intelligence boys began to come to the Farm. Along with the condemnation of anything and anyone German, there had arisen the spy fever. Who was boring from within? Who was flashing signals with news of troop movements to the U-boats off the coast? The German-Americans, of course! And Medford was populated almost entirely by German-Americans, some still speaking with a German accent.

I think Dad sat up nights working up cases against the citizens of Medford. He didn't trust Adolph Hoffman for a minute; Frank Hollman was certainly up to no good; and when it occurred to him that Mr. Zinkeisen had built a concrete tennis court at his rather secluded place south of Medford he immediately leaped to the conclusion that it was not an honest tennis court but a gun emplacement. He saw mysterious lights, and he and the boys from Camp spent many a night pussy-footing around the Selden hills (those vast heights just west of Coram) looking for spies flashing signals out to sea.

I'm sure there were agents at work. I'm sure we needed intelligence and counterintelligence. But I do think that a lot of the goings-on at the Farm and around Medford were pure cops-and-robbers. For one thing, some of the Intelligence boys had no more training for the job than Dad had. There was one who did know what he was doing. He was a New York detective in private life. I can't remember his name but he kept in touch with Hope for a long time.

A quite different lad was one Ray Perkins who was a product of the same world as Irving Berlin. He was red-headed and amusing—a song-writer and singer. He knew he was out of place in the Army and in Intelligence—but how he did love to come to the Farm.

Mother and a home had their charms, and men from Camp Upton often found an excuse to come down to the Farm, sit in the living room and drink the raspberry vinegar that Mother served. This may sound awful but it was delicious, a sweet-sour drink that was very refreshing. I still have the recipe.

Another side of the war came home to us when the hospital at Camp Upton was turned into a center for the long-term treatment of wounded men. Mother discovered that surgical dressings were in such short supply that the old dressings had to be washed and remade and used again. All that gauze came out of the washing process a veritable rat's nest that had to be worked apart, flattened out, recut, and then folded into compresses, rolled into bandages or whatever. An aggravating and time-consuming job. And who did it? The nurses. In their off-duty time. So Mother wangled permission to bring home some of these bags of gauze and she worked them herself, learning along the way how to fold compresses and make up all the odd dressings. She worked quietly and without fanfare but Mother could turn out an amazing amount of such work. When we were home we did our share.

This all entailed many trips to the base hospital and around the wards. She came to know not only the nurses but the men who had been in the hospital for months and would be there for many more months. There were men who had had ten or twelve operations, men who had been in bed for months rigged up with a bottle of Dakins solution, designed to drip on a wound and aid in the healing. Men who were bored and tired of the whole thing. The sight of Mother with her sweet smile and her bright spring dress cheered them to begin with. They were pretty tired of nurses in white and men in khaki and she was a welcome sight.

The care was adequate but the food left something to be desired. No Service food was good in that war. Nobody had heard of dietetics and the Army cooks were not the greatest. Anyway, a lot of these men really needed a little pampering so Mother took this on too. She would pack a basket with biscuits and jars of crushed strawberries and go up to the hospital. A little consultation with the nurses, and the strawberry shortcakes went to the men who were lowest in spirits and needed a lift the most. Soon she was going up several times a week with her goodies. Sometimes there was a special request from a man in bad shape. One of them longed for a piece of roast chicken, one who was very downhearted and totally uninterested in food got a whole meal—light and attractive and smacking of home. She would have fed them all if she could, but had to confine her efforts to the ones who really needed her mothering.

Then she decided they needed something to do as much as something to eat. There was no occupational therapy setup at all. Empty day followed empty day. She further decided that they needed color to feed the soul so she took up a few stamped pieces of material and a bundle of embroidery floss. Not all of the men embraced this opportunity but a surprising number did. Choosing from the feast of colors was a great thing and learning the stitches that Mother taught so patiently was a challenge. Each time she appeared, there was finished work for her, and requests for more. She took the pieces home, finished them off—hemstitching on a towel, lace on a centerpiece—and took them back. Many a family must have been surprised at these accomplishments of Dominic or Raymond.

Rafael Cozenza was her first convert and soon her busiest. He wanted something special for his peacetime boss who was a fish dealer in New York. Dad designed an underwater scene that included all the gaudiest fish in the book. This did keep Rafael busy for a while and made a tremendous hit around the fish market when it was finished and delivered. Finally Mother had to keep some of the pieces and sell them in order to get enough money to buy new pieces and more embroidery floss. She had some wealthy friends who were not only pleased to help but were impressed with the work.

Hope, who was out of school as of June, 1917, dreamed up a bit of therapy on her own—gardening. Things must have been very informal at the hospital for she was given the job of official garden therapist. She lived in the nurses' quarters and she came up with her own uniform—khaki middy and skirt and a great big red tie from Sea Pines days. She had the ambulatory men helping her make gardens between the wards that ran out from central corridors. When they were full of flowers it was cheering to everyone, even those who just walked the corridors.

I daresay these Fullerton operations were among the first attempts at occupational therapy. Eventually the Army organized something with girls in blue and white uniforms called Bluebirds.

Then Mother took on another war job. The LIRR had set up a good-sized establishment at Camp Upton to handle troop movements and supply trains. This

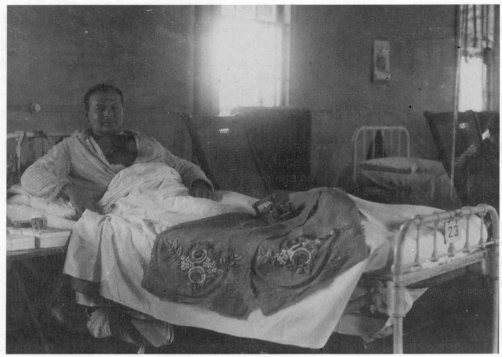

A patient at the Camp Upton hospital with his handiwork, c.1918

consisted not only of business facilities but of living quarters, for this was the end of the line. Men had to eat, and the LIRR Farm was producing food, so Mother set up a canning kitchen in Chiquita Casa and spent many a long hour over a hot stove canning everything she could lay her hands on. I was her assistant in this operation during the summer. We shelled peas by the hour, picked and prepared bushels of beans, canned gallons of tomatoes. Periodically we took loads up to the railroad cookhouse. I have a feeling—I had it even at the time—that all this effort was not really appreciated. I think a brakeman off a freight train would be just as well satisfied with a can of Libby's beans as with the fruits of our devoted labors. But that wasn't the point—the point was to supply food wherever it was needed.

Raising vegetables became a big thing and Victory Gardens bloomed in every back yard. Somebody had the bright idea that the Boy Scouts could do their part in this area and Dad was pounced upon to implement the program. He was a Scoutmaster and a National Scout Commissioner and an easy choice. He immediately picked his own title—Chief Grub Scout—and anyone who didn't know that grub was a good western name for food didn't deserve an explanation.

They inaugurated this Scout program at a giant Boy Scout rally at the Hippodrome in New York. This was the big theater of the day—big enough to accommodate marvelous spectaculars—and I am sure was quite a sight packed with assorted Scouts. Dad addressed them with ringing patriotic fervor and each boy was presented with a package of beans—beans for Victory! I'm sure a lot of these boys did a good gardening job and a lot of families ate better for it.

And then, on November 11, 1918, the war ended. I was at school. We were out at recreation, scattered around the playing fields, when we heard bells in the distance and then cars on the main road honking and tooting as if the drivers were out of their minds. Somebody must have dashed out with the word and all thought of games or anything else was forgotten in the glorious news that the war was over.

We pranced around the grounds, shouting and singing. Girls and teachers alike went slightly mad. Even Miss Faith unbent enough to clap her ladylike hands. Miss Alice—the withdrawn and dignified Miss Alice—jumped for joy like the lowliest freshman.

We all felt it was our victory—that we had all had a part in it. We had worked in our own way and many girls had brothers or cousins or even fathers in uniform. I didn't—except the Chief Grub Scout—but I had taken the whole thing very personally and did a lot of proxy suffering for a lot of people. That seems to be a fault of mine. I have too good an imagination and maybe too soft a heart. I can feel too keenly the troubles of other people.

The treaty was signed in a railway car at Compiègne, near Paris. I saw the spot not too long after. The men got out of the trenches and came home. There were parades and parades up Fifth Avenue as the troop ships came in. We went in to see Pat Tuttle's outfit march past.

He returned to civilian life and he and Hope made plans for their marriage. Pat had raised chickens on the family farm at Eastport and Hope had studied poultry husbandry at Farmingdale so they planned a future in dusty hen houses full of bird-brained chickens and endless brown eggs. As I say—to each his own. They were married in August of 1919. Hope wore the family wedding dress and veil and carried the same gold roses she had for graduation. Jeanette was her attendant. They departed for Flint, Michigan where Pat had a job which was to provide the stake for all those chickens.

Also in 1919, I graduated from Sea Pines and put up my hair.

Guests at Hope and Pat's wedding

HBF, the Chief Grub Scout, c.1918

Après la Guerre

In January of 1920, I went off to Ambler, Pennsylvania, to the School of Horticulture for Women. This school was started around 1910 by a group of Philadelphia women who were advocates of greater opportunities for women and who were also interested in horticulture. As my mother was already actively working in the field, she became involved, and Dad urged them all on.

Dad was way ahead of the times in thinking that women could take their places with men in any field. He was delighted when World War I took women out of the house and into broader fields. Women went into the Navy and became farm workers in the Land Army. They held down jobs in factories and machine shops. My cousin Eunice left her job as a home economics teacher and worked as an auto mechanic in a big garage in Philadelphia.

I had no desire to do anything but pursue work with plants, and I was delighted to go to Ambler. It would have been much better for me to go to Farmingdale or Cornell or any other co-ed school, for I had spent my whole school life among females. Sea Pines was as isolated and self-sufficient as the Farm so I had no experience of studying with, working with, and socializing with the male of the species. I think the folks should have seen this, but they didn't, and I was quite oblivious. Ambler was a good school, so that's where I went.

When we arrived at school on a cold January day, each room had its bouquet from the greenhouse, and when I stuck my nose in the sweet peas and baby primroses (*Primula malacoides*), I felt I was in Heaven. Ambler was a small school—really small. I would guess there were about twenty of us when I went. It was a two-year school so we had juniors and seniors. In another sense, we had juniors and seniors too. We had young women—I was the infant of the school at seventeen—who were planning to go into nursery or greenhouse work, or even

Working garb at Ambler before Eleanor's revolution, 1920

chicken raising. We also had a number of gray heads among us—unmarried ladies of some means who liked gardening and wanted to learn more about it for their own use.

Ambler taught by doing. We had classes in theory and then we went out and worked. Our first day in the greenhouse, we were each given a patch in the vegetable house to prepare and plant with radishes, onions, and lettuce. This was all old hat to me, but several in our class were city girls with no experience in gardens but with a yearning to learn how to grow things. I was astonished at their ignorance and awkwardness, but they got more of a thrill out of their first radishes than I did. We learned to use tools and we made flats, among other things. We each carried our own pocket knife and we whittled out our own dibbles and "little men." These were flat, very smooth pieces of wood that were used for lifting plants from the seedflats for transplanting.

Among Dad's many ideas concerning women and women's emancipation was the matter of clothes. The long, heavy skirts down to the ankle were not his idea of either comfort or efficiency. He had Hope and me in boys' suits when we were young, and he thought the Sea Pines bloomers fine. Then somebody—probably Dad—discovered riding breeches. These, with high-top boots, were indeed made for serious gardening, and that's what I wore. As a matter of course, I took them to Ambler and created a minor revolution.

When I arrived, all the women were wearing work shirts and heavy, ankle-length khaki skirts. Horrible garments for transplanting seedlings in a coldframe, watering a greenhouse or digging a flower bed. They apparently took one look at my neat, comfortable, practical riding breeches and high-tops and made a concerted exodus for Philadelphia and Wanamakers. I think within two weeks the skirts were gone and everyone was striding around in comfort. The gray-haired Miss Reppard from Mississippi and the equally gray-haired Miss Merryweather showed a leg for the first time in who knows how many years.

Even Miss Nicholson, the horticulture teacher, succumbed. She was a great teacher, a Scottish woman who had trained at one of the English horticultural schools. Englishwomen had been training and working seriously in horticulture for years, not only in the daintier forms of the work but as real farm laborers. Two World Wars saw them keeping the country's agriculture going.

This little teacher of ours was as gray-haired as Miss Reppard but with a fresh, young face. She wore a fuzzy Scottish tam on the side of her head and what she didn't know about raising flowers, inside and out, wasn't in the book. She loved her work. I can still see her standing behind the vegetable house and gazing at a newly delivered pile of manure with the greatest pleasure. "That is *beautiful* manure!" was her verdict. A woman who can see the beauty of manure is a real gardener.

Then there was Mr. Doan, who lived in Ambler and came out every day. He taught orcharding and woody ornamentals. The first morning, when our new class was greeted by assembled faculty and school, Mr. Doan approached me and said in his slow, loud, and pedantic voice, "Is this the young lady who once said 'There are no aphids on me'?" All eyes turned in my direction and it was an awfully difficult remark to explain. He must have read Mother's *Lure of the Land* and remembered her quoting a brilliant remark that I had made at the age of four. It seems a ladybug alighted on me and I addressed her thus: "Why, you cunning thing,

Eleanor in her riding breeches and hightop boots, with Donald Ferguson, 1922

do you think there are aphids on me?" Even at that age, I knew that ladybugs prey on the hated aphid. Briefly, I hated Mr. Doan for embarrassing me but he was far too kindly and too knowledgeable in the field of woody ornamentals for me to hold it against him.

Every week, Mr. Doan took us on a field trip for identification work. Usually we went by trolley to the Morris estate in Chestnut Hill. The estate has since become a botanical garden. These field trips were excellent training as we went over and over the same plants until we really knew them. The first one each week was the *Sciadopitys verticillata*, or Japanese umbrella pine, and this name threw a lot of the group right there. I already knew it, for we had one at home. At one point in the tour, we came to the tigertail spruce that Mr. Doan always pointed out gingerly. Its needles were vicious. "This is not well-named," he would say. "It is *Picea polita*, and certainly should be called *Picea* im*polita*." This rated as a great joke with Mr. Doan.

He took us to other estates. We went to the huge Stotesbury estate one day. The gardens were gorgeous, and I slyly pilfered a few slips of boxwood. This had been grown from cuttings of the Mt. Vernon box. I rooted them in the propagating benches at school, along with some plain Ambler boxwood, and took them home to Mother. It is possible that they are still growing at East Setauket.

Mr. Kaiser came from somewhere once or twice a week to teach botany. He also took us out in the fields and woods to learn plants. He had a heavy pocketknife that was always coming out so he could slice off a piece of black birch bark for us to taste, or a jack-in-the-pulpit root for the same purpose. Since this latter contains calcium oxalate crystals that sting the tongue as nettle stings the ankles, this was a great joke with him. We also had classes with him for the book-learning part of botany.

I took all the courses as they came along. I even put up with chickens, and filled incubator lamps and turned eggs dutifully. I didn't get involved with animal husbandry, and beekeeping didn't really interest me, but any kind of work with flowers delighted me and I especially loved the greenhouse work.

I got so involved in the greenhouse work that I eventually dropped the fruit growing and beekeeping courses to put more time on my specialty—and look what happened to me—I married a fruit grower and beekeeper.

There was a three-month break in my senior year at Ambler. I went to France with Dad. On April 27, 1921, I wrote in my diary: "Arriving from Ambler in the morning my family greets me with the question, 'Would you like to go to France?' I decided I would. We went in to Committee HQ and met Miss Morgan and Mrs. Dike. Got my job as secretary to Dad."

Anne Morgan was the daughter of old J.P. and the sister of the great J.P. Morgan, Jr. She was a big, handsome woman with great drive and executive ability. Mrs. Dike was tall and rather willowy and very feminine, but also with drive and ability. She must have had some connections with the French government, for I think it was through her that Miss Morgan was able to establish her Committee.

This was the American Committee for Devastated France. In France it was known as *Le Comité Americain pour les Régions Dévasteés de la France* and was referred to as the CARD. There were other organizations in France, manned by volunteers from the YMCA, the Red Cross, and the Salvation Army, but they worked with the armed forces. Miss Morgan and her volunteers sought to help the battered villages and the villagers. I'm sure there was no trouble in enlisting volunteers for the CARD. As I saw them, they were all girls of wealthy backgrounds, what were then called society girls, and they were ready and eager to do something useful. I am sure they put much of their own money into the work.

When the war ended, the remnants of families returned to what had been their homes and struggled to pick up life again. Miss Morgan rallied all the aid she could get and went in to help reestablish these villages and resettle the people. The government did what it could to clean up the rubble. All the stones belonging to one house were neatly piled and a wide blue band was painted around each pile. Some of these piles were pitiful—hardly enough stone to build a henhouse—and many houses were completely gone. But they would put up what shelter they could, and settle in. Some lived in dugouts burrowed under the shell of the house. But at least they were home.

These were country people and used to feeding themselves. A tiny patch of ground will supply vegetables for a French family, a few chickens or rabbits or pigeons will give meat, and a cow will mean milk and perhaps cheese. But these people came back to nothing—not even a few seeds to *start* a vegetable patch. This was the need the Committee set out to meet. The government gave their blessing, but little more. They had little to give after four years of war.

Apparently, it was the French government that felt the agriculture of the country had received a desperate setback. Miss Morgan appealed to Grace Tabor who was quite well-known as a writer on horticultural subjects. She lived in Huntington and she and Mother were very good friends. She was impressed by Dad's work, and I am sure she felt that reclaiming French battlefields would be just his dish of tea. He apparently agreed, and also welcomed a chance to help modernize European ways in farming and gardening. So he arranged a leave of absence with Mr. Peters and the railroad, turned the Farm and all the current sugar beet experiments over to Mother (who was Assistant Director of Agriculture anyway), tucked me under his arm as secretary and, I think more importantly, as companion, and departed for France.

A French blue Committee uniform was tailored for me. Dad acquired a spruce new Boy Scout uniform. On the face of it this sounds silly, but I think it was pretty necessary to be in uniform if we were to go into the devastated regions, and this was the only uniform Dad was eligible to wear. The Committee was strictly a female operation. The Boy Scouts gave their official blessing through James E. West, the Executive Director and another pal of Dad's.

Ship passage was not easy to come by. Many people wanted to get to France to find their families and help them resettle, and there were ex-soldiers eager to claim their French war brides and bring them back to the States. So when we finally got on board the French liner *Touraine*, we found we were packed four to a cabin.

Among the passengers was one real VIP, Maurice Maeterlinck, the man who wrote *The Bluebird* and *The Life of the Bee*. He was traveling with a third wife— a blond cutie—and two Eskimo dogs. I felt for these lovely creatures being taken to the south of France. I wonder how they fared in that alien climate. My diary mentions the fact that Mme. M. starred in a boxing bout. I don't remember much about this. It must have been by way of entertainment, and it seems to show that Monsieur had not necessarily chosen her for her intellectual attainments.

The *Touraine* was a shabby tub and a bit of a wallower. I was rudely awakened one night when half the Atlantic sloshed in through the open porthole by my bunk. We had run into weather. All the next day, as we steamed past the Scilly Isles and the Lizard, the huge oily waves rolled under us and sent us from one side to the other. The sea was thick with fishing trawlers and they rolled like the proverbial corks. I daresay they came from the little Cornish ports I saw a good many years later—Fowey, Polperro, Mevagissey and the rest. We had a glimpse of the vividly green Channel Islands, made a stop at Southampton, and finally docked at Le Havre.

The train trip to Paris remains a dream of flowering green countryside. Always after a sea voyage, it is the greenness of growing things that makes an impact on me, and this was early May and unscarred French country. The diary effuses over "green alfalfa fields, pink and white apple orchards, gardens of fleur-de-lis and forget-me-nots. And always the rolling hills and the green, green trees and the little cottages with their thatched roofs and walled gardens." And wisteria dripped over every doorway.

We had rooms at the Hotel Star, a pension that was equipped to handle English-speaking strangers. The only time we saw our fellow lodgers was in the dining room. I remember one family group who appeared to be Russian, and I felt sure they were aristocracy escaped from the Revolution. The man was big and rather silent, the woman dark and handsome and elegantly gowned. They had a small boy who ate at another table with his governess. When these two finished their meal, they paused at the parents' table and the small boy kissed his mother's hand. We had fresh sweet cherries and cream cheese for dessert. Now why should I remember that over fifty years?

We saw a bit of Paris, mostly what we could reach on foot. Down the Champs Élysées to the Tuileries gardens and the Louvre was a favorite stroll. The horse chestnuts were in bloom along the boulevards and there were flowers everywhere.

Finally we were taken out to see the agricultural acreage that had to be reestablished. All along the roads there were piles of shells, piles of helmets, and heaps of barbed wire. Death was still in evidence. A cross topped with a helmet—

The village well bears the sign *"Eau Potable,"* near the chateau at Blerancourt.

English or French—was a common sight and there were piles of coffins here and there. The battlefields were untouched, with trenches, shell holes, barbed wire, fluttering shreds of camouflage, spent shells and live shells.

But Nature herself was well on the way to reestablishing agriculture. Weeds and grasses, clover and grain and wildflowers were fast shrouding the mangled land, although they didn't really soften the grimness. There was the little red Flanders poppy, cornflowers and cockle, all in bloom, and also great clumps of star of Bethlehem. With all the talk of the blood-red poppies in Flanders' fields, why did nobody ever mention the star of Bethlehem?

Dad's first sight of this terrain convinced him that it was no agricultural job. It was an engineer's job to clear and level the land and make it ready for the excellent French farmers who could take over from there. The man from the Ministry of Agriculture who accompanied us on this jaunt seemed to feel that the soil had been ruined and that nothing short of scientific miracles would make it productive again. Strange attitude, for it was obvious that the ground would yield again, and even better than before. Where a section had been cleared and planted to wheat, you could pick out every shellhole by the darker growth of wheat. Explosives put nitrogen into the ground. This was one of the advantages of blowing holes with dynamite for planting fruit trees, as Dad had discovered at Wading River years before.

Dad would have enjoyed this challenge if he had been on his own ground, but he was at a fearful disadvantage in France. The language barrier was complete, and when Dad's flow of words was cut off, Dad was defeated. Moreover, in a strange country he did not know his way around or where to turn for equipment. All this got through to Miss Morgan, and I think she saw that our expedition was not going to be fruitful. However, we had brought over a full complement of Planet Junior garden tools with the idea of helping to modernize work methods in market gardens. So we were given a test area to work in and we were to demonstrate the advantages of the push-hoe over the ancestral hand tools.

For this purpose, we were sent to Blerancourt, the Committee headquarters in the Aisne district. The Chateau at Blerancourt had been around for a long time. There were remains of both an inner and an outer wall and remnants of a moat. One of the tombs in the little old church was dated 1022 (that was five years before William the Conqueror was born), so that must have been the era in which the chateau was built, and the village grew up around it.

There was a fine medieval look to the heart of the village. The main street was a solid wall of houses built against each other, with great iron gates giving access to each courtyard. There was a market place and a town hall, and on the edge of town there was the shell of a convent. There was also an archery court that had already been rebuilt.

We had a room in the home of Mme. Descleve. Her husband had been mayor of Blerancourt but he did not survive the war. She and her two daughters had lived during the German occupation in a dugout in the garden, and had done the work of the house for the German officers in residence. The walls were pockmarked by gunfire. Most of the windows were gone and they had been replaced with a heavy yellow paper reinforced with string. The garden had suffered but a few roses had survived.

The village well had been redeemed. Pure water was a big problem. The Germans had poisoned wells as they left and, in the natural mess of war, most were polluted anyway. This was a government job, seeing to it that each village had at least one usable well. The Blerancourt well was just outside our house with its sign, *"Eau Potable."* There was a great clattering of sabots on the cobblestones as the housewives trotted back and forth with their pitchers for drinking water. It was as good a spot for a bit of gossip as ever was Rebecca's well.

The garden space allotted to us was in the Committee garden, hard by the convent. We had not really expected to be on our own. Dad had thought to have a work force, but the whole project had really petered out, so we just did the best we could. We worked up an area and had several demonstrations. One group of Boy Scouts had a Scoutmaster with a command of the English language. Through him, Dad's dynamic personality flourished briefly.

Decoration Day in France was a very moving experience. We went in a body and in full uniform to two American cemeteries, the one at Juvigny and one at

Eleanor pushes a wheel hoe in the garden at Blerancourt. This photograph appeared in the *New York Times*, 1920.

Ploizy, near Soissons. The most touching part of this Decoration Day was the floral tributes. These were made by the local women who ransacked their own gardens, the abandoned gardens, and the fields for flowers. They met in groups and made up wreaths *pour les Americaines*. Mme. Descleve had a group working in the courtyard when we came in from our garden work. What a lovely thing to do for the strangers who lay under their sky.

We had also been assigned the job of taking photographs for publicity use. A photo of me pushing a Planet Junior in the shadow of the convent wall appeared in the *New York Times* rotogravure section. A three-day trip was set up for us to get further afield and for Dad to get more pictures. Our guide and mentor was M. Guerreau, an ex-officer of French artillery, and Dad promptly named him the General—mostly, I think, because his tongue refused the French language and even the word *Monsieur* strangled him.

This trip took us even deeper into devastated France. We had dinner at Rheims and saw the lovely shell of the Cathedral in a golden sunset light. The Cathedral at St. Quentin would have been less than a shell if the Allied troops had not reached it in time. The Germans had left mines with time fuses in the columns. A portion had been restored and we saw a wedding party go in.

It is my humble opinion (as Dad used to say) that World War I was one of the nastiest ever fought. Men lived and fought month after month in trenches—

mile after mile of muddy ditches with barbed wire and land mines to mark off these trenches from those of the enemy across the way. Constant forays across this No Man's Land might result in a section of trench changing hands or just in more casualties.

Now the trenches were finally empty of all but mud, and the barbed wire was rusting among the shell holes. Dad changed his camera plates in many a convenient dugout—and if this was the ultimate in comfort and safety during this war, I can only say the cave man had it better.

And so back to Paris and ten days of writing up reports. We had rooms at the Hotel du Mont Tabor. The General came and dined with us one evening and then took us out to the Bois de Boulogne where, according to my diary, we "went to a sparkly glass and electric light place and sat at a little table under the trees and ate strange coffee things and Dad and the General talked some more...." This was the night life of Paris as I saw it. I remember the Bois more for the lilies-of-the-valley that grew there.

On June 26, we shook the dust of Paris from our heels and left by train for "New York par le Havre." This time we traveled on the *Lorraine* of the French Line, a more pleasant trip and a much nicer and less crowded ship than the *Touraine*. We had fog all the way across the Atlantic. On the Fourth of July, with two lookouts in the bow, we raised land. There was a whiff of green fields and trees mingled with the salt. With the sunset the fog lifted and the Fourth was celebrated by a gorgeous sunset at sea. The diary says, "Dad and three of his assorted friends and I sipped champagne by way of celebrating. Horrible stuff but awfully nice men." One of them was a Lieutenant Baldyga of the Polish army, who insisted that I learn to pronounce properly the name of that stalwart Pole, General Kosciusko.

And so—home. And the final line of the diary reads:

> Ray for the U.S.A.!!
> Fin.

I went back to Ambler and picked up where I had left off. Along toward November of 1921, I was told very formally that I would be given credit for the three months in France and would graduate with my class in December. I had never anticipated anything else. Things usually came my way and I didn't feel I had missed much except in botany. I have a gap where the rest of the class studied the mosses and ferns, but I have managed all these years.

A New Partnership

In January of 1920, a young man had come out to the Farm to apply for a learning job. We had these bright young men most of the time. They came to try out farming, or to learn about some specific field, or to fill in six months before college, or after college, or between years at Cornell.

This young man came from Garden City. His family and Ralph Peters were among the rather exclusive few who lived in Garden City in those days. When he proclaimed his intention of going into fruit growing, Mr. Peters suggested that he serve an apprenticeship with Hal B. Fullerton, who could teach him all he needed to know about fruit growing on Long Island. So he came out, talked with Dad, and it was agreed that he should start work in the spring. And this is the way Donald Ferguson came into my life.

Don was born in 1893, his brother Eric a year later, and they had an older sister, Frances. Their parents were William Cashman Ferguson and Elizabeth Maria Theresa Van Dyck. When Don was only six years old, his mother and sister both died of diphtheria. Two years later, his father married his dead wife's sister, Edith Alina Van Dyck. So his aunt became his stepmother. She had one child, Billy, who died at the age of 15, also of diphtheria.

Don never talked much about his early youth. He was devoted to his aunt-stepmother but he never spoke of his own mother. I really don't think he remembered much. He seemed astonished at all I have dragged from my memories of early days. Donald and Eric were great pals, I know. They were only fifteen months apart and they seem to have been nearly as close as twins. They were constantly together in their young days, and they separated finally in their second year of college.

They were born in Brooklyn and at a fairly early age moved to Flushing. There were social distinctions in Flushing in those days, and Don and Eric and their

Donald Ferguson (right) and his younger brother, Eric, c.1898

friends were known as the rich bugs. There were various rowdy gangs (nice Victorian phrase) of not-so-rich. I take it both these groups looked askance at each other. There was rivalry between the fellow bugs as well as between the groups. I do remember Don talking of top-splitting, which seemed to be very popular. This consisted of splitting the other fellow's top with your own, if you were skillful enough to hit it just right. These would have been the wooden tops with the steel points.

The Fourth of July was a big thing in his young days. He talked happily of the assorted giant firecrackers that both rich bugs and rowdies threw around with wild abandon. He was much pleased when he harked back to the holes they blew in the streets. The bigger the holes, the more successful the Fourth of July. It is a wonder any of them survived to see the dawn of the fifth of July.

Don and Eric sang in the church choir. I believe it was an Episcopal Church. They got twenty-five cents each Sunday and the great sum of fifty cents for weddings and funerals. I'm sure they both looked perfectly angelic in their choir robes—Eric with his innocent blue eyes and Don with his big brown ones.

I don't know when they moved to Garden City but Mother Ferguson used to say there were only three hundred families when they moved there. She also said, every time we drove down Stewart Avenue, that those big maple trees were just at eye level when they drove through with the horse and carriage.

Garden City was a very elegant development—one of the first of the suburban ventures and not at all a development as the term is now used. To point out the exclusiveness of Garden City, when Doubleday, Page & Company decided to establish their publishing business there the community was enraged. Commercialism in their garden town! Actually, the Doubleday Page buildings were as handsome as those of any Ivy League college, and the company built and maintained the most beautiful gardens, open to the public. I walked through them many times, for Doubleday was my mother's publisher and my folks were good friends of Frank Doubleday and his wife Neltje. The latter wrote books on wildflowers and birds which were published under the name of Neltje Blanchan, a name that always took my fancy.

Father Ferguson bought, or built, a cottage at Point O' Woods on Fire Island. They spent their summers there for many years. I heard much about this cottage and the wonderful summers, and in 1924 Don and I went over to spend a couple of weeks there. Don rented a catboat and we sailed away. The only places I had ever seen on Fire Island were the fishermen's shacks that were largely built of wood salvaged from the beach. I knew this was more than that but, after all, a cottage is a cottage. I was indeed taken aback when we got there and I found a three-story house right on the beach. Not only were there accommodations for a large family but there were servants' quarters too. This put a different light on the whole thing and I realized that it had been quite an establishment. There had been Grandmother Van Dyck, Grandfather Ferguson, Father, Mother, and the three boys. I daresay there were guests, too. Who ever had a beach house without guests?

Point O' Woods was as exclusive as Garden City. It was an incorporated community of family homes and one had to be accepted before becoming a part of it. There were a number of Garden City families who went there, and most of the rest came from the more exclusive North Shore areas. It was definitely high class. The men came back from their white-collar days in the city to sail and fish and swim and the ladies sat on their porches and embroidered and rocked and read the kind of books one takes along for summer reading. The maids swept out the sand and made the beds and cooks officiated in the big, airy kitchens.

Provisions came in from the mainland by ferry and were transported across the dunes to the ocean side in little red express wagons. You will find the same wagons on Fire Island still—ideal transportation along the network of boardwalks. Donald never remembered the Home Hampers from the LIRR Farm that he trundled across twice a week any more than I remembered sticking on the label for Mrs. William C. Ferguson at six o'clock that morning. But that was our first contact, tenuous as it was.

Father fished in a dignified manner with the best in fishing equipment. The boys fished anywhere with anything. There was a wreck down west where they went for blackfish, and the bay was full of bluefish in those days, as well as crabs, oysters, and clams. With his big feet, Don was a master clam treader, and this skill he never lost. The Fergusons must have lived very well on the beach.

The boys had wonderful, foot-loose, carefree summers there and ran wild the whole day. They had two small sailboats at different times, the Wood Pussy and the Bellyache. I believe it was the Wood Pussy that they found sunk at its mooring every morning. When they sailed in the catboat races, one sailed while the other bailed. They swam like dolphins. Don became a long-distance swimmer and an underwater swimmer, and he played water polo. He once won a medal for underwater swimming.

When they weren't swimming or fishing or sailing, the two boys would range the beach. Grandfather Ferguson was a serious shell collector who exchanged, bought and sold all around the world. There was one shell to be found on Fire Island that was much sought after by collectors—the pink *Tellina*. The boys were alerted and could spot a pink *Tellina* at full gallop, I am sure.

Even then, Don loved to pick fruit. They picked many a bucket of beach plums and they sailed their catboat east to the Sunken Forest when blueberries were ripe. They found a ready market among the cottages and Don's product sold for a premium, for even then he picked and packed in a masterly fashion. They scored one business coup that he loved to tell about. This was back in the days when the sand bars off Fire Island were a menace to navigation and ships making for New York would often come in too close and run aground. One night, a Spanish ship jettisoned a cargo of lemons in order to break loose and the boys found the beach yellow with them. Early little risers and shrewd little businessmen, they loaded the express wagon and went over to the bay side where they sold several wagonloads before the word got back from the beach that lemons were to be had for the gathering. There must have been vast pitchers of lemonade in every cottage for weeks.

One of Don's compatriots was "King" Noble, a lad who had a tremendous interest in birds. He was a skilled taxidermist and had a license permitting him to shoot any bird at all for the purpose of stuffing it and using it for scientific studies. One of those unusual people who know from early childhood just where they are going, he became Dr. G. Kingsley Noble, Curator of Birds for the American Museum of Natural History. Under his tutelage Don did manage to stuff a seagull, but I never saw this trophy.

When they reached high school age, Don and Eric were sent off to Hoosac School at Hoosick, New York. This was so thoroughly modeled after the English "public" schools that the boys were known as Ferguson, Major and Ferguson, Minor. The classes were called forms, the teachers masters, and at Christmas time they had a great festivity known as the Boar's Head and Yule Log. This entailed medieval costumes for everyone, much holly and plum pudding, and singing of madrigals and lays.

Don never took education very seriously and his recollections of Hoosac seemed to consist mostly of the things they got away with. However, he had five years of Latin and four of Greek and he had a Greek Testament, with an inscription in Latin, that he had won as a prize for scholarship, so he must have done more work than he would admit to.

Donald (left), Billy and Eric at Point O'Woods,
c.1908 *Photograph by Edith V.D. Ferguson*

The boys were in the same class and graduated in 1912. From there, they went to Princeton. Eric did all right and graduated with the class of 1916. Donald did not apply himself here any better than he had at Hoosac, but he thoroughly enjoyed rowing on the freshman crew. He would put the effort and the hours into this that he wouldn't put on his books. I daresay it was swimming and rowing that gave him his great shoulders and upper arms—he was a magnificent physical specimen. So he flunked his freshman year and was sent to NYU for the summer to catch up to the point where he could go back and try again. He apparently reinstated himself and then requested a transfer to Cornell. He had decided that he wanted to be a farmer.

This must have caused real consternation in the bosom of the family. Father was the chief research chemist for the Nichols Copper Company and he had worked hard to reach the status of a professional man. His sons were to be in the same category, either professional men or businessmen. Farming certainly did not rate.

Father decided to cure this young man of his brainstorm and sent him off to Vermont where he made the acquaintance of a Vermont rock farm at East Randolph. This was a one-man subsistence operation. Don pitched in. He was up at dawn, milked the cows, and put the milk through the separator. This was run by sheep-power—an old ewe on a treadmill. Milk disposed of and the utensils washed, he was ready for breakfast. Then the day began—mowing hay with a scythe around and among the rocks, hoeing tomato plants around and among the rocks, digging potatoes—still among the rocks. And when the day's work was done, the cows had to be milked again and the milk separated. Then supper.

He said his hands were so stiff in the morning that he had to work each finger supple before he could manage to dress. But he stuck it out. For all this, he got ten dollars a month plus his keep. I believe the farmer admitted at the end of the summer that Don had done a pretty good job, but really all Don got out of it was a good swing with a scythe and a hearty dislike of cows.

Since this experience had not knocked the farming bug out of his head, his father allowed the transfer to Cornell. Young Donald had decided he wanted to grow citrus fruit. Cornell had no courses in citrus fruit, but that's where he went, took the general ag courses, and got books on citrus growing which he studied on his own time. He left Cornell at the end of his third year and went to California where he worked on a lemon ranch. At the end of three months, he decided this was not his field after all and he returned east.

He then tried his hand at business. He worked for the Lee Tire and Rubber Co. in Conshohocken, Pennsylvania. I don't know just what he did. It seems to have been agreeable enough, but certainly didn't loom as a life's work to him.

Came April, 1917, and Wilson declared war. Don enlisted on April 19. He tried for the Marine Corps but was turned down because of flat feet. He went home and practiced standing on the outsides of his feet to make an arch, and passed brilliantly into the Infantry.

He was assigned to the 5th Infantry and was promptly sent to Panama, where he spent the whole war on Lock Guard. Within a year he was a Sergeant, and was accepted for Officers' Training School. He used to talk about the difficulty of concentrated study in that tropical climate of heat and humidity. This apparently was when he really did get down to studying and he worked the clock around, keeping himself going on gallons of Coca Cola. The exams were grueling and covered everything he should have learned at college. Since he had all the brains any man needed, and finally found it worth his while to use them, he passed, and got his commission in April of 1918. He was transferred from the 5th to the 29th Infantry and made First Lieutenant in August of the same year.

He served as Judge Advocate of special courts martial during that time, and proved himself a good lawyer. A man could choose the officer he wanted to defend him, and Lt. Ferguson soon came to be much in demand. I think he could have been a good lawyer if he had wanted it. He had the right kind of analytical mind.

Don's captaincy was in the works when the war ended that November, and promotions were frozen. Like all our wars, when it was over it really was over, and men were discharged as fast as possible. He was offered a commission in the Regular Army, but he turned it down. He would have done well. He was an excellent officer, as World War II also proved.

He wore his tropical whites in later years when he marched in Fourth of July and Decoration Day parades. It always confused people, for the tropical whites

Donald Ferguson in tropical whites and
Eleanor in her CARD uniform, 1922

were not common. He looked ten feet tall and was always chosen to be Parade Marshal.

Young Donald—not so young now at twenty-six—returned to civilian life with no real plans. I think he tried several jobs, among which was one selling shoes to stores in and around New York City. It must have been at this time that he once more brought up the subject of fruit-growing, and Ralph Peters sent him out to the Farm to talk to Hal B. Fullerton.

When Don came out to the Farm that day in January of 1920, I was home, between Sea Pines and Ambler. I was drying my hair over the hot air register in the living room while Dad and the young man talked at the big table. I was neither more nor less impressed than I was by any of the series of young men who went through the Farm.

I went off to my Ambler career and Don got a job on one of the North Shore estates tending, of all things, cows. He lived at home in Garden City and went back and forth. I don't think he liked cows living in luxury any better than rock-farm cows, but it was a short-term job and he put up with it.

During my summer vacation, we were thrown together in the isolation of the Farm. Don lived in the Postscript with Dad's secretary, Ted Tuttle, who was Pat's brother. They both joined us in whatever we did. There were picnics and swims at the Sound, Grange meetings, and an occasional movie.

When I went back to Ambler in the fall, Don and I started to write. I was always more at ease on paper than in talking, so we developed quite a friendship this way. The next summer was again a pleasant one. Don had a mandolin that he played very deftly by ear and this went along on the beach parties and added to the festivity. He played evenings at home, and he could play along with some of the player piano selections.

In the fall of 1921, Don and I put up the Medford Grange exhibit at the Riverhead Fair. Very artistic it was, and fruit was featured. Of course a Grange exhibit was made up of contributions from all the members, so space had to be allotted to Mrs. Matsunaye's pickles, Andrew Larsen's potatoes, and Mr. Koschara's cabbage, but we managed to give the Farm apples and pears top billing. This was the first time, but not the last, that I did a centerpiece of a cornucopia of fruit and bedded down the plates in kinnikinnick. We only won third prize, but we thought it was gorgeous.

I graduated from Ambler in December of 1921, and in January of 1922 the die was cast and we became engaged. On September 29, we were married under the oak trees in front of the Homestead. I wore Mother's wedding dress and the family veil. When Hope was married she had carried a gorgeous florist's bouquet of roses but I made my own arm bouquet of all the garden flowers I could lay my hands on. There were pale pink asters, lavender scabiosas, little gold dahlias, pale blue *Salvia azurea*. It was a rainbow bouquet because we planned to name our establishment Rainbow Ranch. We went off to Maine for two weeks. A Cornell friend of Don's—Bill McKaye—had loaned us the family cottage on McMahan's

Mr. and Mrs. George Washington McMahan of McMahan's Island, Maine, 1922   *Photograph by EFF*

Don and Eleanor at Rainbow Cottage, 1922

Island, which we reached by way of Bath and a place called Robin Hood. Maine in October is not at its best. We had ten days of fog and it was cold. Moreover, there were forest fires in Canada and the air was full of smoke. I was always on edge when forest fires were around. I did love the deep woods of Maine and the smell of the balsam trees and the strange look of them all festooned with hanging moss.

We got a quart of milk each day from Mr. and Mrs. George Washington McMahan, who had stepped straight out of a Grant Wood painting. This was McMahan's Island so our Mr. McMahan must have been a descendant of the original settlers. Both they and their house looked the part. When we first stopped in for the milk Mr. McMahan was wearing a dock leaf wrapped around his neck. A sure cure for a sore throat, they assured us. I don't remember if it had worked by the time we left.

We came home to Rainbow Cottage at East Setauket. Dad and Mother had bought a piece of land just north of the station and had big plans for the future. Hope and Pat were living in the oldish house on the property and were in the process of building up the poultry business. There was a good-sized field that we were to plant to fruit, eking out with vegetables till the fruit came in. They built a charming little bungalow on the top of the hill for us. Looking well into the future, this was to be their retirement home when we moved on to something larger and they hung up their hats. They named the place Lorelope, putting our three names together—Loring, Eleanor and Hope. Dad designed a logo with an anchor symbolizing Hope, a pigeon (they called me Pigeon Pie), and a rising sun for Loring, who was known as Sunny Jim.

Dad designed the house, supervised the building, and he and Mother furnished it. It was mostly excess furniture from the Farm, but Dad added such touches as the andirons and a little brass kettle to sit on the hob in the fireplace.

The Lorelope logo designed by HBF

(This is a projection in the inner wall of the fireplace, designed to hold the kettle and keep it hot for the next cup of tea—no doubt where you find hobgoblins). This was a sample of how everything was always done for me. It was charming, but I should have been left to do it myself.

The field turned out to be badly infested with quack grass, which is no help in raising vegetables. Don ended up down on his knees pulling it out by the yard. We put up a small stand and we developed a small vegetable business. We had a little greenhouse. This had been a wedding gift from Father Ferguson. It came as sections of sash and it was to be double-glazed, but first it had to be painted. We worked together on it in one of the empty portable houses at the Farm. I could paint but it was up to Don to learn how to glaze. The inner layer of glass was butted and the outer layer lapped, so he had a lot to learn. There was a good deal of broken glass around before he mastered it, but master it he did. The framework for the finished greenhouse was erected by a carpenter, Uncle Peanuts no doubt. He had built the cottage and the garage.

Don did some tree work during the winters. He was an artist at pruning and he did some orchards. He managed the Hoyt farm orchard in Hauppauge one season for a share of the fruit. We certainly lived on a limited budget but we seemed to have what we needed. A Mr. Nilson delivered groceries from his store. He came around once a week with his horse and wagon, took my order, and delivered it the next day. We saw a good deal of Hope and Pat and their small daughter, Frances.

Our firstborn came along in 1923. She was named Edith Eleanor for both grandmothers and two friends, all named Edith, and her mother. She was born at the Farm, and we were cared for by Dr. Beebe (Aunty Doctor) and Nursie Mangan, both of whom had officiated at my birth.

Bruce was born to Hope and Pat just three months after Edith Eleanor and as the two children grew they became the best of friends. They had Taylor Tots (runaround strollers) and they had a marvelous time on Hope's big front porch. It was big enough for great scurrying dashes back and forth. Then they would pause and have long conversations in a language all their own.

Radio appeared on the scene during our East Setauket days. The Radio Corporation of America came into being. They bought vast acreage at Rocky Point and Riverhead, and started to erect their imposing towers. Riverhead was the receiving station and Rocky Point the sending. Dad must have been consulted on the buying of this land as the Army had talked to him when choosing the site for Camp Upton.

General Sarnoff was the guiding spirit of RCA from its very inception, and through this contact with Dad, Pat was offered a job with the embryo company. Feeling that his poultry business was not yet equal to the demands of his family, Pat took the job on a tentative basis. He could always drop out if the whole thing fizzled. But he never did; he went onward and upward as the company bloomed, and ended up as Assistant Treasurer and in charge of their South American operations.

The home radio set appeared. Practically all of these were homemade by would-be electronics wizards. Pat made one and had the thrill of his life when he brought in KDKA from Pittsburgh and WGY from Schenectady. These were the first broadcasting stations that offered music and news and humor—the same menu we have today, but more on the snack-bar level. However, no radio buff was content to get a station and listen to it. The thrill was to bring in another and more distant station. I can still remember the night Pat got Havana on his set.

Then one day Don decided to build a radio. He got the components and whanged together a crystal set. I don't remember what it looked like, but it was the bare bones of a receiving set, I know. A pair of earphones went with it and he nearly turned handsprings when he connected the wires—or whatever—and got good old KDKA clear as a bell. Well, a small, tinny bell, but a bell. We set the earphones in a crystal bowl to amplify the sound and we had dinner music with our hash and string beans. It was a real milestone.

All that remains of the 1750-vintage house at Rainbow Ranch. The new house was built around the old chimney. The Dutch oven is at the back of the largest fireplace.

Rainbow Ranch

We lived for eighteen years and brought up our three children at Rainbow Ranch in Middle Island—as far as I am concerned, the best years of our lives.

In the winter of 1925, Don was employed to look over an orchard that was for sale. He was to report to the prospective buyer on its possibilities. He went over to Middle Island, looked it over, and reported that it was so good he had arranged to buy it himself. I don't think this was really ethical, but maybe it was more honest than giving an adverse report and *then* going out and buying it. His father loaned us the money. A hundred and fifty acres for $15,000. Not a bad buy.

The Randalls, who had once owned the farm, had planted the younger parts of the orchard. They sold it to two "city fellows" who ran it for a few years, enjoyed summers in the country, and had a tearoom for a while in the old house. It was from them that we bought it. Mrs. Randall still lived across the road.

There were some twenty acres in orchard—apples, mostly, but there were a few peaches—a nice old barn, a shed of like vintage, and a little house so old that the floors slanted in all directions and every door had been planed off at a different angle so that it would close. This house had been built about 1750 and had been a Post Office from 1811 to 1835. This goes back to the time when the mail came in by post rider, which gives Middle Island a kinship with the wild west and the Pony Express.

From where I sit now, I realize that this house was an historical treasure and should have been preserved for the ages. But to us, in 1925, it was just an old house with its sills gone and impossible to make livable. We had a living to make and a family to rear, and we wanted a modern house. So the little old house went. We did leave the great, seven-foot-square chimney and built the new house around it. There were three fireplaces, two back-to-back, big enough for five-foot logs, and a third between these two, of later vintage. This one fell apart when we tore the house down, disclosing a Dutch oven between the two big fireplaces. People had been puzzled over the lack of a Dutch oven in a house of this age.

We had to get the house built before we could move, so we sat down and sketched out what looked like a livable house. Mr. Scott of Yaphank was engaged as builder, to Uncle Peanuts' sorrow. Yes, Uncle Peanuts was still in Huntington and still building. He couldn't have built stronger than Mr. Scott but he might have given us a more efficient house, although we were not so far from the time when the height of efficiency was a hand pump in the kitchen sink, as opposed to a well and bucket in the back yard.

The house was built with no help from me. I saw it just once in all the time of its building and Don was much too busy with the orchard to fuss over house details. I was not one to demand a say in it all—I just assumed it would be fine. This was, no doubt, because Dad always attended to such things and I accepted life in a very unassertive way. I hope Mr. Scott appreciated his free rein.

We had a fine big black coal stove in the kitchen with a hot water boiler attached. It did annoy me that things had been so arranged that when one came through the front door into the living room, one's gaze went straight through the archway between living room and dining room and came point-blank against the hot water tank. I felt a lack of the aesthetic here, but didn't see that much could be done about it.

I managed the stove with good enough skill, and it did well by me except when the wind was wrong and it wouldn't burn right. Then I could be frustrated, but mostly I was quite fond of it and refused to part with it when we eventually left the farm. I was going to have it in use again someday, and I took unkindly to gas and electric stoves.

I used Mrs. Potts sadirons to iron our clothes. We had used them back at Medford, too. These irons did a good job but were a bother. They had to be heated on the coal stove, even in July. A detachable handle shifted from one iron as it cooled to a nice, fresh, hot one. You tested the heat with a wet finger and learned to tell by the hiss if it was hot enough. You also tried it on the end of the ironing board cover to see if it was too hot, not on the best linen table napkins.

We had a coal furnace in the cellar with a hot-air heating system. Don ran the furnace like an old master, and a coal furnace takes skill. We used the fireplace in the living room from November to May. Don made fires there that would have roasted an ox and it was God's grace that we didn't burn the house down, for that chimney was the one built in 1750, and mortar and bricks are not immortal.

We had a telephone from the beginning. It was a wall phone with a crank that we spun to raise the operator. Several neighbors were on the same party line. We each had our own ring, and everybody knew when anybody had a call. Our number was 75F11, and the ring was one long and one short. There were a lot of people who monitored all calls on the line. Our neighbor Mrs. Randall was one of these,

The living room fireplace at Rainbow Ranch   *Photograph by EFF*

and she would be upset when she was at our house and another number rang, for I didn't believe in listening in. This left gaps in her knowledge of her neighbors' doings.

We did not have electricity. We hadn't had it at East Setauket either, so we were twelve years without it. We had kerosene lamps that sufficed nicely. I hated to clean and fill them, and was prone to leave the job till supper time, which meant that I took rather kerosene-smelling hands to the stove. The big table lamp went from the living room table behind the loveseat to the middle of the dining room table for supper. This doesn't make the ideal centerpiece, and we always rejoiced when spring advanced to the point where we could have supper without the lamp. I have never quite recovered from that. It is still a great day when we have supper by daylight. It was about 1935 when the power lines finally came through on Middle Country Road and we all hooked up. Our house had been wired when we built it, so it was not much of a job.

It must have been late winter when we bought the place and Don was all agog to get in a full season's work. The orchard had to be pruned and the brush cleared away. He was at Middle Island all day every day. He got hold of a young man in the neighborhood to work for us. This was Al Cattle. Don wanted an all-around farm worker but also one who was good with machinery and Al was highly recommended as a "good hand with cars and such." He was more knowledgeable than Don, but he was rather what Dad called a "bale-wire mechanic." It is the wonder of the world that these two ever kept tractor and sprayer and water-pumping system functioning long enough to get the work done. It was standard procedure for the sprayer to break down just as they got out to the orchard with a full tank.

If it wasn't the sprayer that went to pieces, it would be the well. I had spent my life with broken well rods at Medford and the subsequent joys of keeping house with what water you could haul in from the neighbors. Dad was never so happy as when they were fishing for the rods. If well rods break so often, I never could understand why they weren't so constructed that they could be raised without days—yes, literally days—of fishing. Dad enjoyed this, for he loved an emergency, and he loved solving problems, but it drove Don mad. He had no patience with inanimate objects and wanted only to get on with the raising of fruit.

The cider operation was another bale-wire setup. It was in the old barn on the rise behind the house. The barn was really another museum piece. It must have been built at the same time as the house, for it was put together with wooden pegs, and I'm sure had had hand-split shingles. The cider press sat on the dirt floor of what must have been the cow stable, and the tractor that ran it was hooked up outside the back door. Cider making is a sloppy job anyway, and this got really sloppy. Besides that, it got cold along in November.

The whole neighborhood was interested when we bought the farm. They took a very dim view of us at first. They were quite frank in predicting that the rich man's son would fall flat on his face and give up fruit growing in short order. I'd love to have heard the predictions around the coal stove up at Pfeiffer's store. But the talk died down, and we were eventually accepted in all kindness.

It was old Mr. Bayles next door who scoffed loudest. He had a front-row seat, as their house stood higher on the hill and looked down on our place from the west. He had a poor opinion of both city fellows and rich men's sons. The name of Richard M. Bayles is well known among Long Island historians, for he wrote several books on Island history. He was a real patriarch of a man—tall and stooped and with long white hair and beard. The most kindly of men, but the kids stood in awe of him. They called him "The Big Man." His wife, "Grandma Bayles," was a sweet little robin of a woman who loved all children. She remembered the days when the schooners plied Long Island Sound and came in on the tides to load cordwood.

Richard M. was a surveyor, which was a good occupation for one dealing in history, and he was a printer, so he could print his own books. He had an office next to the house and here were his presses and his fonts of type. Some of this equipment is at the Carriage House Museum in Stony Brook now, in the print shop. So fast does today become yesterday and history. He was an insurance agent also, so Richard M. had many strings to his bow.

He had two sons. Thomas was married and he and Gertrude and their sons, Elwin and Donald, lived in quarters that had been built onto the office. I think this was supposed to be temporary, but it became their permanent home and they seemed quite content and comfortable. The second son, Albert, lived at home and remained a bachelor all his life. He was a carpenter and hammered many a nail into the barracks at Camp Upton in both World Wars. Eventually he gave up this work, took over the insurance business, and did a little printing on the side.

Mrs. Randall lived alone and was the complete and typical country woman. Her house was as neat and clean and stark as a hospital ward. She had a big garden and loved flowers. When we knew her, her active gardening days were over and she just enjoyed the perennials that ran wild on her hillside. Coreopsis blazed gold farther and farther afield every year as it seeded its way along, some little old iris survived, and a peony or two, but what I remember mostly was the phlox. This had seeded as exuberantly as dandelions and had run out to the worst and most awful magenta shades.

Like all country women, she was generous in sharing her garden. She would come over along toward fall with handfuls of phlox seed and scatter it all through my flower beds. What could I say? She must have wondered why phlox didn't "do" for me, for I pounced on every phlox seedling as it showed its innocent head and yanked it out. But she was a kindly, friendly neighbor.

The Bayles place had been carved out of the old Randall farm so our land adjoined theirs on three sides. I envied Gertrude in the spring, for she looked out of her kitchen window into our blooming orchard to the west. I had to walk back through a patch of woods to see and smell apple blossoms. Not that it was a hardship, and I did it often.

I would walk back to the orchard in all seasons with the kids, but especially at apple blossom time. Then we would pack up our lunch every day and go back to eat under a pink and white apple tree ahum with bees. I think this was Don's idea. This was a grand time for him, with early spraying done, a respite before the petal-fall spray, and the whole prospect of a bumper crop spread before our eyes. A good bloom is a gorgeous sight. Of course there are many disasters that can hit between bloom and picking basket, but your hopes are high in May. The fragrance of the apple blossoms and the hum of bees is still with me along with the joy of our whole family in our own orchard.

Don was never really a farmer for that includes all the many facets of life on a farm, including the proper care and feeding of machinery, but he was a wonderful

Apple blossom time at Rainbow Ranch   *Photograph by EFF*

fruit grower. He had learned much from his two years at the Farm with Dad, and he read and studied. When the fruit came in from the orchard there was no doubt that he knew his business and when we put on an exhibit at one of the fairs there was no handsomer fruit to be seen.

Our ultimate effort came when they offered a prize at the Mineola Fair for a display fruit exhibit. The best of our fruit moved into the living room and Don spent a whole day and a whole night packing. I had grown up on fairs and it was nothing new to me to have the entire living room floor paved with the choicest apples so that a bushel of the super-choicest could be selected and packed. Don packed bushel boxes and bushel baskets of apples and sixteen-quart baskets of peaches and pears and crabapples. He prepared specimen plates of each variety— five perfect, matching specimens on each plate.

We set them up at the Fair, and I filled a cornucopia with the loveliest fruits I could find, setting a rosy peach against a golden Winter Banana apple, a striped Gravenstein in a nest of purple-bloomed Hyslop crabapples. And then we bedded down the whole exhibit in kinnikinnick, just as we had done for the Grange exhibit back in 1921. This was an old trick of Dad's, to tie an exhibit all together with a background. I can still show you the spot on the Coram-Port Jefferson road where the kids and I gathered all the kinnikinnick.

What beautiful things the apples were, and what a joy to work with. Everybody had a favorite variety and the kids were as choosy as anyone. A Delicious eater would pass by the McIntosh or vice versa. I had different cooking uses for different varieties. Through the season I moved from one to another. Of the summer apples I liked Ohio Nonpareil and Summer Rambo—two of our really old varieties. Ohio Nonpareil made a pale, smooth, tart applesauce, while Summer Rambo sauce was darker and more meaty. Both were good, but it was the Rambo I used for pie.

The best apple pie in the world is made with Gravensteins, preferably Red Gravensteins. I early decided I'd have to learn to bake a good apple pie if I was going to live by, and with, apples. So I kept at it till I did achieve a reputation for being a good pie baker. Actually, the family had no other pies to compare, so they became addicted to my ways with them.

Ours was an old orchard and we had some very old varieties. In this day of rediscovering and preserving old varieties, that orchard would be a treasure. Some trees must have been fifty years old, a newer section was half that age, and Don planted still more. He cleared a piece north of the main orchard and put in Cortlands. This was a new apple at the time—a cross between McIntosh and Ben Davis. A most unlikely cross, but it was a marvelous apple. The fruit was flattish-round and of a deep, dark red, with that lovely bloom that dark red fruit assumes. The flesh was white and crisp and firm. They were wonderful to eat raw, made a good pie, and baked beautifully to a white puff of softness. They are still a favorite of mine.

The Ben Davis was a very old apple and one valued for its keeping qualities. True, they would keep forever, and be as undentable in June as they were in October. Don always said they "had the rich flavor of new-mown cork." There was a little old lady who ran a boarding house in Yaphank and she bought Ben Davis from us "because they keep so well." Our Ben Davis were among the old trees and Don could see no purpose in giving them houseroom, so he grafted them over. It took him at least three years but when he got through he had Stayman Winesap and Delicious instead of corky old Ben Davis. This was a real satisfaction and money in the pocket.

We had an early tomato crop that was really precious. This was what farmers call a "catch crop." It fitted into the complicated schedule of raising fruit. We had the advantage of being able to start our own plants in the greenhouse, which we had moved from East Setauket, and they were at least in bud when they were set out. When winter pruning was done, there was time to get the greenhouse going and start the tomato plants. When the early spraying was finished and there was a pause for the orchard to bloom, the tomatoes were set out in the field behind the barn. This was a high spot, fairly safe from the late frosts. Then in July, when spraying was finished for the season and the fruit was developing, the first tomatoes ripened. Like everything Don raised, they were super tomatoes and he developed a super pack and got a super price. When ordinary tomatoes brought seventy-five cents a basket, Don got three dollars.

When the first good summer apples came in—the Ohio Nonpareils and Rambos—we opened the stand. This was just a series of steps on a table with a roof overhead supported on cedar posts. I think Dad was responsible for this, and he designed the Rainbow Ranch sign. Don also had a giant red apple constructed of metal and this hung out closer to the road. It certainly caught the eye and it became a local landmark.

From July to the end of November, the stand was the focal point of all farm life. This was where the fruit moved out and the money moved in, and what we took in during those five months was our yearly income. By the following June our resources were mighty low and everybody needed new shoes. But of course by June all three kids had given up shoes and they ran barefoot all summer.

The stand season started quietly with tomatoes and early apples, but then came peach season. From late August through September it was a madhouse. People came from far and wide for our peaches. We started the season with Golden Jubilee and Cumberland, the former spicy and yellow, the latter white and pink and so mellow and sweet that it was a sin. Sliced together and topped with cream stolen from the top of the milk bottles, they were heavenly eating. Then we went into Hale and Elberta and Belle of Georgia, the main crop. These came in for the Labor Day season when all the summer people packed up and went home in time for school. They *all* stopped at Rainbow Ranch for peaches. Then people settled down to canning and they all came back to get some more.

The roadside stand and the red apple at Rainbow Ranch   *Photograph by EFF*

We went into the good fall apples like McIntosh and Cortland. Fall Pippin and Maiden Blush were two of the fine old varieties of fall apples. People were ready to make pies again with the lazy summer days behind them, and kids needed apples in their lunch boxes. So every day was busy and the weekends horrendous. It took all of us to man the stand.

In early fall, the kids gathered black walnuts from our many trees, spread them in the ruts of the farm roads and let the truck husk them as it hurtled from orchard to storage cellar to stand. This was their racket, and they had the money from the sales.

I made jams and jellies through the summer and fall, and this was my racket. My desk was bought with one year's proceeds. Since I made some 1500 glasses in a season, this apparently didn't net me a great deal. I made raspberry and currant jelly, which brought me the patronage of Mrs. Otis of Bellport. She eventually took all I could make. She was the widow of the Otis elevator man and she traveled around in basic black and pearls, with an attendant companion and a very nice driver.

By late October we were into Delicious, York Imperial, Baldwin, and Rome Beauty, and the cider season opened. We would close up the stand just before dark and move the fruit to the storage cellar. This was a mad race with the last of the daylight, for there was no light in the storage cellar. All kids rallied for this wild loading and unloading, and the late customers continued to clamor. We kept a few jugs of cider on the front porch, and any apples that had been ordered and paid for, but after dark we were through.

Supper was quite often baked beans (hot out of the coal stove oven), lots of bread and butter, and applesauce. Then we all collapsed in front of the fire and counted money. I would unload the cash box periodically during the day and bring in handfuls of bills which I cleverly concealed among the books in the bookcases. Don always had an excellent idea of what the take should have been, and more than once I had to hunt out another book and its cache.

November was the month for winter apples. It could be slack during the week, but the Sunday drivers swamped us. Thanksgiving brought a great demand for cider. By then we were about out of apples, even cider apples, so we closed the stand. In December and January I went back to housekeeping and Don started the pruning and planning for the next season. A couple of times he went over to the Bellport Coast Guard Station on Fire Island for wintry vacations. He walked the three miles across the bay on the ice. The Captain was an old friend from Point O' Woods days, a bayman with generations of baymen behind him. Don would walk the beach, gather skimmer clams for the cook, watch the rum-runners making for the Inlet, and thoroughly enjoy himself. The men came over once a week for supplies which they transported on sleds and we would meet them on the beach at Bellport. They looked like a group of Eskimos coming across the ice.

In the early days, I was responsible for the stand. We did not have a steady stream of customers then, and I could go about my housework and keep an ear cocked for the sound of a car horn. This was not too bad until our second, Anne Van Dyck, came along in 1927 and it was a bit difficult if I had her in the tub or was nursing her. The poor child's lunch was interrupted more than once. When she was born and I was in the hospital for ten days, Badger came out from New York to keep house for Don. As noted earlier, Badger was my grandfather—my mother's father—John Alonzo Jones. He had always been handy around the house, and he liked to cook, so he volunteered to come out and supply three meals a day.

He helped on the stand too, and developed a real interest in the operation. He was a striking old gentleman, a good salesman, and had a way with people. The customers liked him and readily bought the "straight Baldwin" cider that he kept behind the stand for "special customers." In actuality, this was the cider that was beginning to bubble in an interesting way. Don always told people frankly what it was, and many preferred it when it had achieved a bit of sparkle, but this was not Badger's way. He was a bit of a con artist. We were so amused by him that we let him have his fun. By 1930, when William Cashman was born, we had regular help on the stand and life was simpler for me.

The three children had a fine life. They had free range of the whole farm— 150 acres of woods, orchards, and fields—as well as all the woods surrounding us. When they were small I kept them within sight, but that still gave them all the area they needed for their small doings. As they got bigger, they rode the truck back and forth to the orchard and raced among the trees. They went off by themselves into the woods and explored. In the spring they found arbutus and lady's slippers, in the fall Indian pipes, and in the winter wintergreen berries and ground pine for Christmas decorations.

We always had a dog who was at their heels all day, and this was a good life for a dog, too. It is only in these days that a dog leads a dog's life—penned in the house, taken out for necessary walks on a leash, and never a chance to race and sniff and explore the world. Our dogs spent the whole day exploring.

I feel strongly that this is the best way for children to grow up. On a farm they have all the time they need to grow, internally as well as externally. As plants need nourishing soil, sunshine, and sufficient moisture to bring them to maturity, children need surroundings that nourish the soul, and time—the slow, sure time of Nature—to develop their personalities. I had this kind of childhood and I know full well that sitting in a violet bed and *feeling* was far more constructive than were the music lessons and the dancing classes.

There was always something going on, from the first turning of the soil in the spring—disc-harrowing the orchard and the field behind the barn where we raised the early tomatoes—to the first ripening fruits and on to the final picking of the last apples. Occasionally, when the kids got bored, they would go out and hunt for black widow spiders. We were fairly well supplied with them, but they lived under rocks and in other such secretive places. Sometimes they were found in empty apple boxes that were stacked conveniently in the orchard, and once I found two in a basket of peaches that had been left by mistake in the orchard overnight. Don liked creatures like this, and he kept black widows in match boxes. You learn awfully fast to open a match box cautiously. Nobody ever was bitten.

Although the kids had free run of the orchard, they also knew the rules, which meant no picking of fruit from the trees. Windfalls, yes, but not the perfect fruit. There were two exceptions. In the middle of the main orchard, near a stone pile, was an old Red Astrachan tree and a Yellow Transparent, and these trees were theirs. They were early July apples that came in before the stand was open so they were quite expendable. We had our share of applesauce—and nothing smells better than that first pot of applesauce simmering away on the stove—but mostly the kids ate them. They scrambled through these two trees and reached and picked and crunched like so many squirrels.

This had been my joy at Medford—to sit in a fruit tree and eat. It came hard to me to forego that pleasure on our own farm, but I could readily see Don's point. This fruit was our living, and also it was his pride and joy. Just once, I rebelled. Rufus Seward, an old friend from Sea Pines, was visiting, it was peach season, and I announced to Don that we were all going back and eat peaches off the tree. He was too shocked to protest and we all marched back—Rufus, the three kids and I—through the woods to the peach orchard. And eat we did. This must have satisfied me for I never did it again.

In January of 1934, we had the blizzard to end all blizzards. Long Island was not noted for heavy snows, and the highway departments were caught unawares. They had trucks and they had the snowplow attachments, but in most cases the plows were not where the trucks were, and the drifts were so high that they could

The three young Fergusons, Bill, Anne and Edith, c.1934

not get to the snowplow sheds without the plows. A real stalemate. It was ten days before our road was cleared, and it was a state road. Somebody broke through with horses sufficiently so Don could walk down to the Stewarts for milk. No mail came in and no traffic moved.

Don shoveled away around the back door and the kids managed to get out and wallow in snowdrifts. Billy was so small he couldn't manage it so he slid down drifts on his stomach. We had a pantry and cellar full of food, the results of my summer's canning, and the potatoes we always stored. There was coal for the furnace and the stove, wood for the fireplace and kerosene for the lamps, so we were quite self-sufficient. With such deep snow it was impossible to work at the pruning, so we were all in the house together. It was lovely. We read and played games, Don played the mandolin, and Edith and I picked at the piano. There is much to be said for the togetherness of a blizzard.

School could have been a real problem to us, as it had been for my folks at Medford. We were in the East Middle Island school district. When we moved there, it was a one-room school, unchanged in the quality of its teaching as it was unchanged in the quality of its amenities. The former was provided by the teacher the school board could get cheapest; the latter consisted of a wood stove, a bucket of drinking water with a dipper, and an outhouse.

Progress crept in just in time for our children. A new school was ordained by the County Supervisor and Don worked his way onto the local school board. The new school had two classrooms, an office, an auditorium, plumbing and central

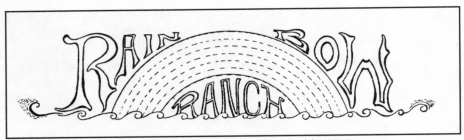

The Rainbow Ranch logo designed by HBF

heating. Two rooms meant two teachers and the cost of the whole operation was outrageous to the diehards and to the old-timers who had no children to consider and went, anyway, on the old theory that what was good enough for Grandpa was good enough for them. Don soon became Chairman of the school board and held the job for twelve years, which got our three through elementary school. He held out for good teachers at a decent salary but it wasn't easy. There were fair teachers, pretty good ones, and one really great one—Ruth Jones.

Ruth Jones deserves a whole chapter to herself. She was a lovely person of the caliber to teach in a select girls' school, but she had fallen in love and married Tobe Jones, a fruit grower in Yaphank, so her lot was cast in the rural areas. Ruth loved teaching and she had a wonderful feeling for children. She gave the youth of Middle Island more than the three R's—along with a sound elementary education, she gave them a touch of culture.

When we moved to Middle Island in 1925, high school didn't enter into the picture at all. The State was responsible only for elementary education. Occasionally, young Middle Islanders with ambition and ability aspired to high school, but in this they were on their own. First they had to convince their parents, some of whom considered it sheer nonsense. Many of the parents had emigrated fairly recently from Poland. They were fine people and hard-working farmers and they eventually came to see the value of schooling for their children, but in those early days they could not always see much beyond hard work—by the age of fourteen, a boy was ready to pull a man's weight on the farm, and a girl was helpful both in the house and in the fields.

Once the hurdle of parental permission was surmounted, a girl—they were mostly girls, as I remember—had to find a place to stay in Patchogue, for there was no commuting. A job as a mother's helper usually worked out, and I think these young people must have gotten more out of high school than the resident pupils because they wanted it enough to fight for it, and that's a great incentive. Again our timing was right and our children went to Port Jefferson High School, courtesy of the School District.

Although Middle Island in our time was populated largely by Polish farm families, it had been a spot on the map since Colonial days. Middle Country Road carried what traffic there was from the west end of the Island to the eastern settlements. The Hallock Inn in Smithtown and the Old Horn Tavern out at Ridge testify to this—they were the night stops for the stagecoaches. And there were old houses to prove it had been a community—the Ritch's place west of us, and our own old house. In fact, the old house that we acquired and, alas, pulled down was one of three built by the Hutchinson brothers. The one at the foot of our hill, behind two big white pine trees, was known as "the house where Cynthia Hutchinson hanged herself." I never heard why. That house was lost to a gravel company, as our place eventually went—sold for a fabulous sum for a gravel pit.

The third Hutchinson brother built still further east of us, at the top of the next hill. This house was owned by Ed Pfeiffer in our day. Mr. Pfeiffer ran a typical country store and acquired the Post Office, so he was quite busy. One went there for the mail, a loaf of bread, a gallon of kerosene, and perhaps a horse collar or a pair of work shoes. He carried them all. He also had one of the early gas stations and it was here that we gassed up on the trips from Medford to Wading River in the IHC days.

Mr. Pfeiffer was a small, wiry man who talked in a husky whisper. He had been kicked in the throat by a mule (or was it a horse?) in earlier days, and I guess he was fortunate to have any voice at all. He had married one of the many school teachers who came and went in the little school. Between them they ran a tight ship. If you asked for a pound of sweet potatoes, you got a pound—if they had to cut off an inch of sweet potato to achieve it. School teachers never lasted long in rural areas. A sure way to find a husband was to take a rural school.

Among the old Middle Island families were the Rulands, the Randalls, the Stills and the Swezeys. There were our neighbors, the Bayleses, and the Van Horns who lived in another of the really old houses east of us. In fact there were two Van Horn houses. Two maiden ladies lived in a once-charming little house on the shores of Artist Lake. That one just disintegrated and disappeared after they died. The other, belonging to brother and sister Marion and Violet Van Horn, was moved when the road was widened. It quietly collapsed during the moving, so Marion had to build a new one.

Then there were the Bubbs on Bartlett Road, and Aunt Minnie Ashton in the very ancient Ashton house next door. There was a story about hiding the family silver behind a brick in the Ashton chimney to keep the raiding British from finding it at the time of the American Revolution. Adam Bubb came from "out east" and he married Jerusha Munsell, whose family was related to the Ashtons and was equally old. In fact, it was the Munsell Road that ran through the middle of the Medford Farm. Adam raised vegetables and had a route out in Eastport. He would bring back a load of ice, so he also had an ice route. He supplied us—a bit erratically—and we were thankful for ice in the icebox most of the time. Their daughter Beth and I became very good friends. Mrs. Bubb talked much of Brother Than, about when he "went to war" and "after he came back from the war." It was some time before I realized that Brother Than's war was the Civil War.

We had other friends on the Bartlett Road, none other than the Bartlett ladies. These were two maiden ladies of fairly advanced years. Agnes was tall and thin, Maud shorter and decidedly plump. When we first knew them, the children had a little difficulty with their names but Billy figured it out—Miss Agnes was the one with the lavender teeth. They were an interesting pair with an interesting background. They were Brooklyn aristocracy and their father had been a judge. He owned many acres of land in Middle Island. There was a back road that went through this property which Dad had found years before and liked to use. Like me, he much preferred a back road to a main one. There was a row of tumbledown sheds along this road that Dad said had been slave quarters. I'm not at all sure of this, but they may have been of the same vintage as the house, which was indeed old.

I have no idea if this was old family property or was bought by the Judge but, as far as I know, it was only used as a summer residence. They came out by LIRR, of course, and the train stopped for them at the Bartlett Station. I daresay this was a whistle stop like the Farm. Now it is just a spot on the railroad about a mile east of the Farm where the Bellport Station Road crosses Long Island Avenue.

They were forced to come down in the world when the Judge died and it was found that he had very little to leave to his wife and two daughters. All those acres and acres of land, but not much in the bank. The girls, however, decreed that Mother should never know and that she should continue to live in whatever lap of luxury she knew. So, by the time Mother died, there was even less for the girls, and luxury became a thing of the past. They had their house on Pierrepont St. in Brooklyn—one of the old Brooklyn brownstones—and the Middle Island acres with the house there. This was a very old house and quite large for the age in which it must have been built—around the early 1800s, I would guess. It was little changed when I knew it, and it is gone now. After their deaths it stood empty, and eventually was so vandalized that it was torn down.

Julia Muirhead had run the tearoom in our little old house. She was a cousin of one of the city fellows. Later she set up in an equally old house in Coram. She was very successful, for she attracted ladies who had the leisure to drive from Syosset or Bayshore or Quogue for a cup of tea and a piece of the fabulous orange cake that Julia made. The Southampton-Montauk crowd stopped en route. From west to east and back again, one had a choice of Montauk Highway or Middle Country Road. There was no Expressway and no Sunrise Highway, so going through Coram was as easy a way as any, and Miss Muirhead's Orchard Tearoom prospered. She even served Eleanor Roosevelt one day, and to her she confided the secret of the orange cake. Nobody else ever got it.

Another highly successful establishment was the Dutch Oven Inn. Badger was tired of the city and the New York flat, and was still too young—at eighty—to quit working, so he conceived the idea of building and running an eating place. Albert Bayles helped him with the heavy work of framing, but he finished the rest himself. He built the Dutch Oven Inn around a replica of the Dutch oven in our

Badger's Dutch Oven Inn, closed for the winter   *Photograph by EFF*

house, and his menu consisted mainly of dishes he could bake in this oven—baked beans, nut bread, and apple pie. He also served clam chowder.

He developed a small, enthusiastic clientele who found his place attractive and interesting, his food good, and Badger a fascinating character. Nobody knew him as plain John Jones. I don't think any of his customers would have believed that his name was not really Mr. Badger. John Jones just did not fit that striking, white-haired, white-bearded old gentleman. He told a good story and, like my Dad, was not averse to making a good story better. There were many long, leisurely lunches down there, and Badger's Dutch Oven Inn did quite well.

Loring also established a business on our property. He had gone to Michigan State University to study forestry although, in spite of his upbringing on the Farm, subjected to the endless preoccupation with growing things, he cared nothing for plants and the last thing in the world that interested him was forestry. However, he had become a good runner at prep school and he was all for going on to a college track team, and Michigan State had a good track team. He became captain of the track team and a 4:21 miler. And then a strange thing happened. In the course of pursuing forestry, he ran into landscape design and discovered that this was for him. He must have absorbed a lot by osmosis all those years on the Farm, for he became wonderfully knowledgeable about plant material and became as good a grower as a designer.

When he decided to have a nursery and landscape business of his own, we let him have the ten-acre field at the back of our property for his nursery stock. He patiently built up his stock and began to get landscape work as well as maintenance work. He lived with us for seven or eight years and became a very solid part of the family.

Hal B. Fullerton at age 68

Endings

Life fell apart for Dad when his work at the Farm was done. From there on it was all downhill. In 1927 he retired and he and Mother moved from the Farm to our cottage at Lorelope in East Setauket. They planned to run Lorelope Nursery, in partnership with Hunter Sekine. Mr. Sekine was Japanese. His English was sketchy, but he and Dad managed to communicate. He bowed from the waist to Mother and he always brought her gifts—strange teas that tasted like alfalfa to our Occidental palates, and a red silk piece embroidered with peonies.

His past seemed very shadowy, but Dad gathered that he came of a high caste family. Apparently he had been a war correspondent during the Russo-Japanese war and was on the staff of a Japanese newspaper over here. He had acquired a place in West Yaphank and there he planned to raise choice Japanese ornamentals. His little old house took on a distinctly Japanese aspect, and he eventually had a vast number of flowering cherries, wisteria with yard-long blooms, and tree peonies. According to Dad, some of his stock came from the Emperor's own gardens, but between Mr. Sekine's difficult English and Dad's imagination, I would not guarantee this. Mr. Sekine was to raise the stock for Lorelope Nursery and Dad and Mother were to market it.

It never worked out. Dad had no business ability, they knew nothing about running a nursery, and they had no capital to work with. Apparently, Dad had never thought of making provision for the time when salary became pension and the LIRR was no longer there to pay the bills. And he was, all of a sudden, too old and too tired to make a new start.

Mother had become the Farm's Director of Agriculture after Dad's retirement. She carried on the work for a short time till the Farm was closed down and then the LIRR gave her an office and a job in New York. She must have seen that the nursery business was not going to get off the ground, so she worked to make something of the New York job, commuted for a while from East Setauket, and then accepted an invitation from friends to stay with them in New York. She died in 1931 and we put her ashes under the big oak tree on a hill behind the Dutch Oven Inn.

Dad left the cottage at East Setauket and came over to live with us. He helped on the stand in the early part of the season and he loved the kids, a feeling that was completely mutual. He died in 1935 at the age of 78, and we put his ashes under the same oak tree.

As for Badger, his daughter Catherine, my mother's half-sister, came out from New York after she was widowed and she lived with him year-round. He gave up cooking in the Dutch oven, and kerosene stoves turned out the baked beans, but the oven was still a fine conversation piece. He slowed down over the years and when World War II cut down on the use of gas for pleasure trips his trade fell off. Eventually Aunt Catherine was barely keeping things going. He continued to slow down and he died at the age of ninety-two.

World War II crept up on us gradually, as it did for the whole world. Slowly but inexorably, it reached out for us all. In mid-1941, the Army Air Corps (predecessor of the U.S. Air Force) came to Don with a request to organize an aircraft spotting post. The newly formed Ground Observer Corps consisted of a network of spotting posts all along the eastern seaboard, each manned by civilian volunteers who reported every aircraft flying over. Sightings were reported by telephone to a Filter Center where aircraft movements were tracked on a map. The purpose was to provide early warning in case of a possible German suicide strike against our coastal cities.

So Don rallied half a dozen young fellows and decreed that the field across the road from the stand was indeed a spotting post. It was manned for a few hours now and then when the Air Corps planned to send out flights for the sole purpose of being spotted. In 1941 air traffic was not what you could call congested. The boys had to run across the road to our house to phone in their reports on the party line. It was Don who made the first report—a flight of B-10s in the south.

Then came Pearl Harbor and the whole United States went to war. The enlistment centers were mobbed, the young men disappeared, and old men, very young men, and women came forth to take over the home front jobs. And the Ground Observer Corps went on around-the-clock duty. Thanks to those few dry runs, there was an organization to call on, and a few who knew what was expected of them and how to do it. Don was Chief Observer and got it all organized.

It is a matter of great pride to me that I took the first wartime watch of Dudley-92. For a few days, all we had was a post in the ground with a board on top to hold the reporting forms. Then a shelter was thrown up and then a windbreak of brush. Loring called this the Boma. Any good African knows that a boma is a defensive enclosure. Ours was a defense against the north wind.

Eleanor and Don in 1943, after Don returned to
the Army during World War II

Finally, a small building contributed by the Highway Department was
erected higher on the hill, west of the Bayleses, and we used the phone in the Bayles
kitchen. A wood stove appeared. Eventually we had a direct phone line to the Filter
Center. In time, Donald Bayles built us a tower that took us some thirty feet up in
the air and gave us much better coverage. A twenty-four-hour, seven-day-a-week
schedule was worked out and men, women, girls and boys came from Coram and
Selden as well as Middle Island to serve their two, or four, or six hours a week. As
service-age men disappeared, other people took over.

The day after Pearl Harbor, Loring put down his pruning shears and digging
fork and enlisted in the Navy. Nobody had any false ideas of this being a short and
easy war, and nobody made plans for "after the war." So Loring sold his hard-won
nursery stock for a fraction of what it was worth and went off to become one of
the first radarmen. He was a member of a Navy beach battalion and took part in
the amphibious landings at Gela in Sicily and at Salerno on the Italian mainland.
He returned stateside for officers' training and then was sent to Guam where he
was involved in top secret communications.

Sometime during the spring of 1942, Don announced that he had to get back
into the Army. I made no protest for I saw how it was with him. He had already

talked of selling Rainbow Ranch and going into small fruit somewhere on the North Shore. He had been trying out raspberries and had become fascinated with them. When we went to Middle Island, I had expected to spend the rest of my life there and I asked nothing better. I loved the place, and I loved the work, but I could see how he felt and had accepted it.

I took over the spotting post and was Chief Observer for six months. Don hired George Lymber to run the farm and George did manage to get the crop in. By then, all the help we could get was high school boys. It was a case of doing the best you could with what you could get. I knew there would not be another season for us at Rainbow Ranch, so I settled for just getting through this one and getting the place sold.

And that was not easy. It was not the time to sell a farm. Eventually, Leo Lentin came to look at it—a most unlikely prospect. He had a very fine dress store in Patchogue, and why he wanted a farm was as much a mystery to the friends who came with him as it was to me. But Leo had, apparently, a love of the land, and he wanted a farm. Moreover, he could well afford it. So he bought our 150 acres for $15,000—the same price we had paid for it.

We spent the rest of the war years moving from one rented house to another, first on Long Island and later in Upstate New York. The greatest wrench for me was leaving my garden. When you have spent eighteen years building up a flower garden, your roots are as deep in it and as firm as those of the phlox and the lilacs. The only way I could manage was to ignore it the whole spring. I just wouldn't look at the crocuses and tulips.

I did succumb to taking a small clump of the little English sweet violets with me—those white and pale lavender ones that were my very first memory at age three. So perhaps this is a fitting place to end this book of memories.

Epilogue

After the War, Eleanor and Don returned to Long Island. Don taught fruit growing and beekeeping at the Long Island Agricultural and Technical Institute in Farmingdale until his retirement. They moved to St. James where they raised raspberries, bees and flowers until Don's death in 1971 at age 76.

Loring became a fine landscape architect and moved to New Jersey where he died in 1973. He and Dorothy had no children so this line of Fullertons has "daughtered out."

Hope served in the WAC from 1944 to 1948. She and Pat parted and she was remarried to Air Force Sgt. Joseph Zarensky. In her later years she became a much-published poet. She died in 1990 at the age of 91 leaving two of her three children (daughter Jean died in 1966), 13 grandchildren, and 12 great-grandchildren.

As for the three Ferguson children, Edith is a highly skilled weaver living in northern Vermont with her husband, Henry House. Anne is a science writer, editor and retired biologist living in southern Nevada with her husband, Charles Nauman. Bill spent 30 years in the U.S. Air Force and retired as a full Colonel. After the death of his wife, Julie, he was remarried to Bette Mankin and moved to Port Angeles, Washington, where he died in 1988.

In 1979, Eleanor moved to Vermont to be near Edith. Of course, she also moved a clump of her violets. In 1993 she celebrated her ninety-first birthday. Although she is in frail health, she remains robust in mind and spirit and participated wholeheartedly in the preparation of this volume. In collaboration with Edith, she recently published a book of her verses, *It's Good to Be Alive*.

Eleanor remains the acknowledged family matriarch to her two surviving children, 10 grandchildren, 20 great-grands and one great-great-grand. She is a family treasure to the grandchildren, for whom she was truly a fairy-tale grandmother during their growing-up years.

A.N.